1/01

Secrets of

HYPNOSIS

D1593262

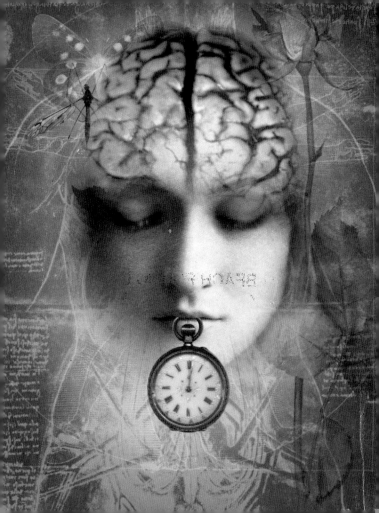

Secrets of

HYPNOSIS

JANET FRICKER
AND JOHN BUTLER

A Dorling Kindersley Book

Dorling DK Kindersley

LONDON, NEW YORK, SYDNEY, DELHI, PARIS, MUNICH and JOHANNESBURG

This book was conceived, designed, and produced by
THE IVY PRESS LIMITED,
The Old Candlemakers, Lewes, East Sussex BN7 2NZ

Art director Peter Bridgewater
Editorial director Sophie Collins
Designers Kevin Knight, Jane Lanaway
Editor Rowan Davies
Picture researchers Liz Eddison, Vanessa Fletcher
Photography Guy Ryecart
Illustrations Sarah Young, Catherine McIntyre, Vanessa Luff, Andrew Milne
Models Mark Jamieson

First published in The United States of America in 2000 by
DORLING KINDERSLEY PUBLISHING, INC.,
95 Madison Avenue, New York, New York 10016

Natural Health ® is a registered trademark of Weider
Publications, Inc. Natural Health magazine is the
leading publication in the field of natural self-care. For
subscription information call 800–526–8440 or visit
www.naturalhealthmag.com

Copyright © 2000 The Ivy Press Limited

A CIP Catalog record for this book is available from
the US Library of Congress.

ISBN 0-7894-6776-3

Originated and printed by
Hong Kong Graphic and Printing Limited, China

see our complete
catalog at
www.dk.com

CONTENTS

Mysterious process
*The practice of hypnosis
partly works by tapping into the
subconscious workings of the brain.*

HOW TO USE THIS BOOK
Hypnosis is not something you can practice easily on your own at home; beginners will need an experienced therapist to set them off on the right track. For this reason, *Secrets of Hypnosis* gives advice on how to find a suitable therapist, removes the mystery of hypnosis by telling you what you can expect from a typical session, and covers the range of medical and psychological uses to which hypnosis can be put. There is a chapter dealing with the special uses of hypnosis when dealing with children, and throughout the book there are case studies illustrating the range of benefits clients can obtain from hypnosis.

Important Notice
Hypnosis is not an appropriate therapy for physical problems that require a medical diagnosis. It is also unsuitable for certain serious psychological problems, such as psychosis and endogenous depression. Since the effectiveness of hypnosis depends greatly on the client's confidence in the therapist, it is important to select someone who is reputable. Check that your therapist is a member of an established body before starting treatment.

SLEEP TEMPLES The best known of the ancient links to modern hypnosis are the sleep temples of the Egyptians, Greeks, and Romans. Egyptian sleep temples, located along the Nile River, appeared around the fifth century BC, and were dedicated to the fertility goddess Isis, who was also believed to possess healing powers. The subject of a ritual was put into a deep sleep by a priestly magician, during which he was believed to reveal himself and offer both diagnosis and treatment. The sleep cult spread to Greece with the construction of the Temple of Asklepios during the fourth century BC. As many as two to three hundred are believed to have been built. Asklepios was the Greco-Roman god of medicine and was thought to cure the sick in dreams.

Healing Techniques
The induction techniques used in the sleep temples closely predicted the methods developed later, and are particularly reminiscent of the techniques used by Franz Anton Mesmer (see pp. 14–15). They included the laying on of hands, the use of physical suggestion, the losing of visual attention and the use of rhythmic chants and musical forms. Greek versions of healing gained entrance to the Temple of the sacred sleep room – after cleansing themselves physically through bathing, and spiritually by making offerings to the gods. While no teachings were acknowledged by many members of Greek society, a number of intellectuals raised the question of fraud.

Healing chants
Curses were thought to be induced by the laying on of hands by priests.

Sweet dreams
In the temple, patients would try to summon the appearance of Asklepios, who gave treatment instructions.

Color therapy
The temple walls were painted in different colors, considered significant in the healing process.

History
*The first part of the book takes you
through the evolution of hypnosis.*

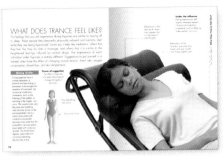

WHAT DOES TRANCE FEEL LIKE?

The feelings that you will experience during hypnosis are similar to those of drifting off to sleep. Most people feel pleasantly physically relaxed and mentally alert while they are being hypnotized. Some say it feels like meditation; others that they flow like they do after a massage; and others that it is similar to the heightened feelings induced by certain drugs. The experience of each individual under hypnosis is entirely different. Suggestions to put yourself in a relaxed state have the effect of changing muscle tension, heart rate, oxygen consumption, blood flow, and skin temperature.

Rating Under
...

Power of suggestion
...

Under the influence
...

Demystify
The second part of the book shows you what to expect when visiting a hypnotherapist, removing any fear of the unknown.

Health benefits
These spreads explain the health and psychological benefits which you can gain from hypnosis.

Asthma: Prevention Through Imagery

The lungs
...

Asthma is a condition in which the airways in the lungs become inflamed and are sensitive to specific triggers that cause them to narrow, reducing the amount of oxygen reaching the lungs and resulting in coughing, and shortness of breath. Sufferers include police, exercise, or household mites. It is one of the most common chronic illnesses, affecting around 7 percent of the population. Studies have shown a fourfold increase in the number of children suffering from asthma over the last 20 years, but the reasons for this are debatable.

The effects of stress
While stress does not cause asthma, psychological factors can exacerbate the condition. Strong emotions like anger, stress, or joy can trigger an attack. Older children and adults sometimes find that the asthma gets worse at times of stress, such as during an argument. Suffering a severe asthma attack is in itself very stressful. When an attack occurs, hyperventilation is accompanied by anxiety, which aggravates the breathing problems, which can result in a vicious cycle of escalating symptoms.

It should be noted that hypnosis is a conventional treatment and should not be used in an acute attack in which life-saving medications must be administered.

Hypnosis has a role in promoting general relaxation, and in the exploration of underlying anxieties which are known to exacerbate the condition. Relaxation can reduce the incidence and severity of asthmatic episodes, and self-hypnosis can alleviate asthma at the start of an attack. Here, visual imaging of the expansion of the airways can be used. Hypnosis is not appropriate, however, when someone is in the throes of an attack. To suggest to an asthmatic patient that she is not wheezing (which can make symptoms relaxing and endangers breathing).

Medical studies have demonstrated the benefits of hypnosis in lessening the occurrence of asthma attacks. A year long study of 15 asthmatic patients who were taught self-hypnosis showed that their admissions to hospital were reduced from 44 in the year before, starting therapy to 13 in the year after. (Morison, 1988)

Preoccupied
...

PTSD: CASE STUDY
Fiona, a 32-year-old businesswoman, was involved in a major rail accident. She was uninjured but saw many distressing scenes. At first she experienced profound shock, for after a few days she began to lead a little better. Suddenly two weeks later she started having graphic flashbacks to which she reliced the event in intense detail. These happened both when she was asleep and when she was awake. They came to dominate her life to such an extent that she felt she couldn't concentrate on anything else and stopped going to work. She became withdrawn from her husband and friends, who she felt had no idea what she was going through. Her husband felt that her character had changed overnight, and had no idea how to help.

Survivors
...

The nightmare...
...

Case studies
Case studies which demonstrate the practical applications of hypnosis may be found throughout the book.

Introduction: Consciousness and Hypnotic Trance

Everyday occurrence
Superficial hypnotic states and experiences are commonplace and not much different from daydreaming.

Hypnosis is defined as a state of consciousness in which your logically analytical faculties are reduced sufficiently to allow deeper levels of your subconscious mind to be utilized for the benefit of your health. A hypnotic trance is a state of "focused concentration" in which you are neither fully awake nor fully asleep. Deeply relaxed people are open to suggestion, and can be desensitized to fears, phobias, or pain. Hypnotized subjects can be virtually oblivious of what is going on around them, yet are acutely aware of a narrow range of stimuli called to their attention by the therapist.

Trance consciousness

Levels of consciousness range from states of alertness to sleep, with daydreaming, a moderate trance, and a deep trance lying in between. There are no rigid boundaries between the levels. For example, when you are alert you will be running, when you are daydreaming you will be thinking about running; in a moderate trance you will imagine yourself running, in a deep trance you will physically feel yourself running; and when sleeping you will feel that, to all intents and purposes, you are participating in the race.

These types of trance states are quite familiar to most people. You experience these states when you daydream or become so absorbed by a novel or movie that you are totally unaware of other things going on around you.

Hypnotic techniques are used subconsciously by many people in their everyday lives. Suggestion, distraction, relaxation, and visualization are used routinely by doctors, salesmen, and advertisement designers, without their subjects ever being aware of it. Even mothers routinely use the hypnotic suggestion "I'll kiss it better" to ease a child's pain.

Hypnotherapy

Hypnosis has moved away from its earlier association with quackery and is gaining acceptance within the medical establishment. It is used in fields such as medicine and sports to change the way a person's brain interprets experiences and produce a change in perception and behavior. The application of hypnosis for therapeutic purposes is generally called hypnotherapy.

HYPNOSIS
AND HISTORY

Hypnotism has had a checkered history, and still suffers from an image problem. It has been tainted by the exploits of some stage hypnotists who have used it for degrading public entertainments, and by the works of novelists such as Charles Dickens and George du Maurier, who portrayed hypnosis as an occult force. Today, hypnosis is fast gaining credibility as a valuable medical and psychological tool, with many orthodox doctors now referring patients to hypnotherapists. ◦ Virtually every human being, unless mentally disabled or psychotic, is capable of entering a hypnotic trance. The big advantage of using hypnosis as a treatment is that it is without side effects. ◦ If you are anxious about trying hypnosis you should be reassured that you cannot be made to do anything against your will that is unacceptable to your own values and patterns of behavior.

What Can Hypnosis Do for Your Health?

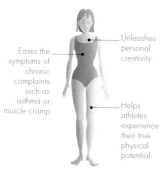

Unleashes personal creativity

Eases the symptoms of chronic complaints such as asthma or muscle cramp

Helps athletes experience their true physical potential

The many uses of hypnosis
Hypnosis benefits the body on both mental and physical levels.

Hypnosis has been found to be effective for a variety of problems that hinge on the emotions and habitual behavior, even in cases involving the body's involuntary responses. While it will not cure underlying physical disorders such as cancer, heart disease, or infection, it may help to boost the immune system and can reprogram our attitudes toward illness.

Medical uses

Hypnosis can be used to relieve virtually all types of pain. It is used to treat chronic pain caused by arthritis and back problems, for example, and, almost unbelievably, as a natural alternative to anesthesia during operative surgery.

Hypnosis can be used to ease symptoms, reducing the effects of chronic problems such as irritable bowel syndrome, asthma, and eczema. Dentists also use hypnosis to calm a fearful patient or ease the discomfort of dental surgery.

Psychological uses

Hypnosis can be helpful against anxiety, tension, depression, phobias, and compulsions, and can help to break an addiction to smoking, alcohol, or drugs. By giving suggestions, therapists can build up positive feelings about being a nonsmoker and a revulsion for the taste and smell of cigarettes. For phobias, hypnosis can be used to reduce or overcome anxiety so that the patient can learn normal adjustment. This may be done by engendering a vivid image of the phobic situation in which the person is relaxed, helping them to adjust their reaction to the feared situation habitually into a normal, calm response. Hypnosis can be used to take people back in time to undo a trauma, by providing an opportunity to reframe events.

Creative uses

Hypnotism has many creative and performance-enhancing uses. It can be used to refine athletic performance, providing strong focus and increasing muscular endurance.

In areas such as the performing arts, hypnotic techniques can also be used to release blocked potential. They may also help students to retain facts for academic examinations.

HOW DOES IT WORK?

Hypnosis is now a well-recognized scientific phenomenon, but there is still no accepted definition of what it constitutes. Some scientists speculate that it prompts the brain to release chemicals called enkephalins and endorphins, natural mood-altering substances that can change the way people perceive pain and other physical symptoms. A more popular view is that hypnosis involves the left side of the brain (the conscious mind) switching off and the right side of the brain (the unconscious mind) being allowed to run free.

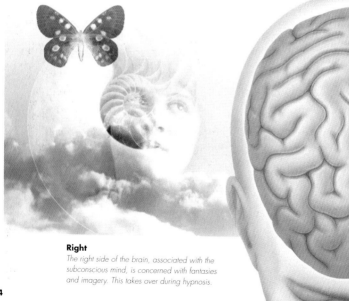

Right

The right side of the brain, associated with the subconscious mind, is concerned with fantasies and imagery. This takes over during hypnosis.

The left side of the brain

According to Professor John Gruzelier, a psychologist at Charing Cross Medical School, London, the way to induce the hypnotic state is to provoke the left side of the brain to switch off, allowing the right side of the brain to take over. This can be done by making the brain focus on something monotonous such as a droning voice or a watch swinging on a chain. Once the left side realizes there is nothing worth attending to, it hands over to the right side.

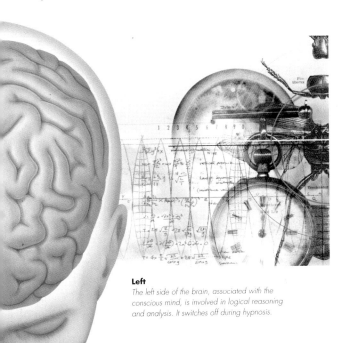

Left

The left side of the brain, associated with the conscious mind, is involved in logical reasoning and analysis. It switches off during hypnosis.

How to Find a Good Practitioner

Know your practitioner
*One of the most important aspects
of hypnosis is to ensure that
you visit a reputable therapist.*

Y ou need to remember that
hypnosis is a powerful tool. While
techniques like visualization and
basic relaxation can be tried when you
are alone at home, you should not try to
treat serious medical or psychological
problems with self-hypnosis alone and
without consulting an appropriately
qualified health-care professional. Just as
you wouldn't take pills without proper

knowledge of what it is that you
are taking, you shouldn't experiment
with hypnosis.

There are some, quite rare, cases
of hypnotic interventions performed
by untrained practitioners causing
temporary upset to subjects, where the
use of inappropriate suggestions has
stirred up deeply buried traumas,
causing extreme anxiety.

Credentials

Unfortunately, in most countries there
is still no official regulation of
hypnotherapists to help you make your
choice of practitioner and feel confident
that you have selected someone
reputable. In the UK, for example,
anyone can practice or even set up a
training school with an impressive-
sounding title. In other countries there
can be even greater confusion, with the
situation varying from nation to nation.
In the US, for example, the state of
Indiana has passed legislation requiring

hypnotherapists to have at least 350 hours of professional training, while most other states have no such legal requirement.

It is always advisable to check that your therapist is a member of an established and reputable body before starting treatment. Checking on the credentials of your therapist is important not only to confirm their good reputation, but to ensure that the therapy is effective—unless you have a good deal of confidence in your chosen practitioner's abilities, hypnosis is unlikely to work for you.

Caution

No practitioner should ever claim to cure serious physical disorders, and hypnosis should never be used as a replacement for medical treatment. Likewise, even though it works with the mind, hypnosis is not recommended in the case of psychological problems caused by chemical imbalances in the brain, such as psychosis, endogenous depression, or antisocial behavior.

WHAT TO LOOK FOR

Ideally, you should choose a hypnotherapist who has been personally recommended to you by someone you know and trust. Alternatively, you could ask your family doctor for a recommendation, or contact one of the organizations listed on page 219 for a list of reputable therapists in your area. Before choosing a therapist, decide whether you would feel more comfortable with a man or a woman. When you contact them to book an appointment, make sure they have some experience in treating your particular condition.

Research

In order that you can feel comfortable with your therapist, be prepared to ask them some questions on your first meeting.

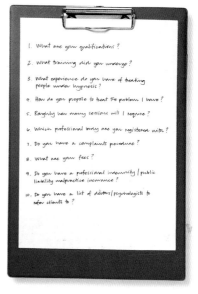

1. What are your qualifications?

2. What training did you undergo?

3. What experience do you have of treating people under hypnosis?

4. How do you propose to treat the problem I have?

5. Roughly how many sessions will I require?

6. Which professional body are you registered with?

7. Do you have a complaints procedure?

8. What are your fees?

9. Do you have a professional indemnity / public liability malpractice insurance?

10. Do you have a list of doctors / psychologists to refer clients to?

Creating a Rapport

Before beginning therapy it is a good idea to speak for some time with the therapist to determine whether you have personal rapport with them and confidence in their knowledge. If you feel anxious, ask if you can take a friend along for the consultation. Any therapist who refuses such a request should be viewed with caution. When you go for the first consultation, check whether the consulting rooms are reasonably quiet and private. Doors banging and people shouting can be very disruptive during sessions.

The therapist

A therapist's personality is almost as important as their professional qualifications—they should make you feel at ease.

The client should be willing to discuss sensitive issues

The therapist should make you feel relaxed

Early Uses of Hypnotic Techniques

Historical
Hypnosis has long been considered an effective medicinal device.

The concept of using trances to alleviate illness recurs throughout the history of medicine. Over 4,000 years ago the founder of Chinese medicine, Wang Tai, used words as a healing tool, and hieroglyphics on Egyptian tombs from 3000 BC record a form of hypnosis. The oldest written record of hypnotic cures was obtained from the Ebers Papyrus, which describes practices used in Egyptian medicine before 1552 BC. This describes a physician placing his hands on the head of the patient and, claiming superhuman therapeutic powers, giving forth strange utterances or suggestions which resulted in cures. King Pyrrhus of Egypt, the emperor Vespasian, Francis I of France and other French kings up to Charles X also practiced healing in this manner.

Hippocrates, the Greek physician, referred to as "the father of medicine," is also known to have discussed the phenomenon, saying "the affliction suffered by the body, the soul sees quite well with the eyes shut."

Hypnosis in the Bible

In the Bible the first recorded use of hypnosis according to some is to be found in Genesis 2 v.21–22: "So the Lord caused a deep sleep to fall upon man, and while he slept took one of his ribs and closed up its place with flesh."

In this incident, God used hypnosis as an anesthetic so that Adam felt no pain during the removal of his rib. In the book of Acts, there is a reference to an apostle gazing into the eyes of a person and healing them. "This man was listening to Paul as he spoke, who when he had fixed his gaze upon him, and had seen that he had faith to be made well, said with a loud voice, 'Stand upright on your feet.' And he leaped up and began to walk." (Acts 14 v.9–10.)

Some believe that the sleep of Saul (I Samuel 26 v.12) and Job (Job 4 v.13 and 33 v.15) was similar to a hypnotic trance. Others believe that Jesus induced trances in many of the people he healed.

Hypnosis in battle

Genghis Khan, the thirteenth-century Mongol ruler, used group suggestions on his warriors to inspire them to feats of bravery in battle.

SLEEP TEMPLES

The best known of the ancient links to modern hypnosis are the sleep temples of the Egyptians, Greeks, and Romans. Egyptian sleep temples, located along the Nile River, appeared around the fifth century BC, and were dedicated to the fertility goddess Isis, who was also believed to possess healing powers. The subject of a ritual was put into a deep sleep by a priestly magician, during which Isis was believed to reveal herself and offer both diagnosis and treatment. The sleep cult spread to Greece with the construction of the Temples of Asklepios during the fourth century BC. As many as two or three hundred are believed to have been built. Asklepios was the Greco-Roman god of medicine, and was thought to cure the sick in dreams.

Healing Techniques

The induction techniques used in the sleep temples closely paralleled the methods developed later, and are particularly reminiscent of the techniques of Franz Anton Mesmer (see pp. 24–5). They included the laying on of hands, the use of physical magnetism, the fixing of visual attention, and the use of rhythmic chants and musical forms.

Greek seekers of healing gained entrance to the Abaton—the sacred sleep room—after cleansing themselves physically through bathing, and spiritually by making offerings to the temple. While the healings were acknowledged by many members of Greek society, a number of intellectuals raised the question of fraud.

Healing rituals

Cures were thought to be induced by the laying on of hands by priests.

Sweet dreams
In the temple, patients would try to summon the appearance of Asklepios, who gave treatment instructions.

Color therapy
The temple walls were painted in different colors considered significant to the healing process.

Leading the Way in Hypnotic Therapy

Franz Anton Mesmer
Arriving in Paris in 1778, Mesmer and his "animal magnetism" gained a cult following.

Modern hypnosis commenced in the eighteenth century, when a flamboyant Austrian physician named Franz Anton Mesmer (1734–1815) arrived in Paris and went on to develop the theory of "animal magnetism." Portrayed by many of his contemporaries as a charlatan, Mesmer is now regarded as a pioneer in the development of hypnotism, and psychotherapy.

Science or scandal?

Mesmer believed that illness resulted from imbalances in the body's magnetic forces, which he could restore to health by transferring magnetism from his own body to that of the patient. He endeavored to achieve this with magnetic passes—long, sweeping movements of his hands that skimmed the surface of the patient's skin without actually touching it. After a period ranging from a few minutes to over an hour the subject would sink into a mesmeric "trance" or "coma."

Mesmer called the force "animal magnetism": He believed it affected the nervous tissue of the human body. After treatments people swore that they had been cured from diseases ranging from blindness to rheumatism. What Mesmer apparently failed to grasp was that his artistry produced self-hypnosis, which helped patients to use the power of their subconscious minds to elicit a cure.

Facing the sceptics

Mesmer's downfall was that he craved recognition, not just from the masses but also from the scientific establishment. He was widely unpopular in conventional medical circles because the growing popularity of animal magnetism was largely at the expense of more orthodox practitioners. Sceptics persuaded King Louis XVI to appoint a Commission of Inquiry, to investigate claims of animal magnetism.

The Commission asked Mesmer to magnetize a cup of water, and then secretly switched it for an ordinary cup. When a woman was given the water she produced classic signs of trance. The Commission concluded that Mesmer was a fraud, and that imagination rather than magnetism was responsible for all his cures.

Although Mesmer left Paris in disgrace, his followers continued with the practice, dropping the more theatrical trappings of treatment.

Irresistible force
Mesmer mistakenly attributed the success of his treatments to the forces of magnetism.

EARLY TREATMENTS
Several writers have left vivid accounts of Mesmer's salon in the Hotel Bullion in Paris. Here he created a mystical atmosphere using lighting, music, and many mirrors, since he believed that animal magnetism could be reflected. Subjects were seated around the legendary "baquet," the apparatus that Mesmer had devised for storing animal magnetism in order to treat large numbers of people at the same time. The baquet, or wooden tub, contained iron filings and bottles of magnetized water from which protruded a number of moveable iron rods. Holes around the top allowed subjects to reach through and grasp the iron rods to receive the "magnetic flow." To help the circulation of magnetic fluid, everyone in the room linked hands.

The crisis
When obstructions to magnetic fluid were cleared the result was a "crisis" where patients laughed, cried, or fainted.

Esdaile's Method

The Scottish surgeon James Esdaile (1808–1859) performed more than 250 operations, such as amputations of the limbs and the removal of tumors, using mesmerism as the sole anesthetic. He discovered that when he mesmerized a patient to get rid of the pain, any redness and swelling disappeared too. The method might have survived had it not been for the discovery of chloroform.

Figure of fun
Mesmer experienced early successes, but later in his career he was widely ridiculed.

Pioneer
With hindsight, it is possible to see Mesmer as a forerunner of modern hypnotherapists.

A New Wave of Scientific Interest

British developments

James Braid induced the hypnotic state by asking people to stare at a fixed point for a few minutes. He also gave us the swinging-watch method.

Interest in the healing properties of trance were resurrected by James Braid (1795–1860), a Scottish ophthalmologist working in Manchester, who in 1841 coined the term "hypnosis" after the Greek word for sleep—*hypnos*. Braid's interest had been aroused by seeing a performance of mesmerism. He believed that the phenomenon was due to the property of the nervous system, which if exhausted, gave rise to the hypnotic state.

Although Braid's neurological theory was erroneous, he based it on physiological and anatomical facts, using scientific jargon. This gave his work credibility with scientists.

Investigations in France

After Braid's death, interest waned in Britain, but in the last quarter of the nineteenth century hypnotism began to gain the attention of a number of respected scientists in France. Most prominent of these was the French neurologist Jean-Martin Charcot (1825–93) from the Salpêtrière Hospital, who had responsibility for a ward containing a number of hysterics. It appeared to Charcot that hypnosis was similar to hysteria, because many of the hypnotic phenomena he elicited by suggestion were similar to symptoms of hysterical disorders.

Charcot made the fundamental error of teaching that hypnosis was a pathological condition that could only be induced in those who were psychologically disturbed. Charcot's pupil, Pierre Janet, developed hypnosis, regarding the artificially produced state as a condition of "dissociation" in which one part of the mind functions independently from the other parts.

Auguste Ambroise Liébault (1823–1903), a medical doctor, and Hippolyte Bernheim (1837–1919), a professor of psychology at the University of Nancy, were the first to regard hypnosis as a normal phenomenon that was psychological in origin. They believed it could be used therapeutically.

As the nineteenth century came to an end, interest in hypnotism declined. Ironically, this coincided with the recognition of hypnosis in 1892 by the British Medical Association as a therapeutic agent.

SIGMUND FREUD

At the end of the nineteenth century, neurologist Sigmund Freud (1856–1939) saw mentally-ill patients being hypnotized at the Salpêtrière Hospital in Paris. This experience became a major inspiration behind the development of his theory of psychotherapy. The way the patients behaved under hypnosis revealed to him that under our day-to-day consciousness is another level of consciousness that affects our behavior without our knowing it. Although he was not the first to make this observation, Freud recognized the "unconscious" mind as a major source of psychopathology.

The Key to Memories

Unconvinced
Freud found hypnotism unhelpful, saying that it was impossible to predict whether a patient was susceptible.

Freud rejected the use of hypnosis as a tool to unlock repressed memories. One factor in this choice was that Freud was not skilled in the art of trance induction. He also believed that the relief of neurotic symptoms by hypnosis did nothing to help the patient understand the nature of their symptoms, and left the causes of the neurosis untouched. His distrust of psychotherapeutic procedures, which he saw as based on authority rather than rational analysis, may have been behind this view. Freud's new methods of psychoanalysis contributed to a general abandonment of the use of hypnosis at the beginning of the twentieth century.

In psychotherapy, patients lie on a couch and talk freely about whatever comes into their mind

Pedigree

Freud studied under Charcot at the Salpêtrière and worked with Janet, making him conversant with the techniques of hypnotism in use at the time.

Psychoanalytic therapy

Psychoanalytic therapy was developed by Freud to explain the personality and behaviour in terms of unconscious wishes and conflicts. The personality is seen as being composed of the id (which drives the individual towards pleasure), ego (that mediates between internal desires and reality), and super-ego (derived from moral and social standards indoctrinated by parents).

Hypnosis in the Twentieth Century

Walking wounded
Soldiers at a field hospital in Meuse, France, during World War I. Hypnotherapy was widely used to treat returning soldiers.

During the First and Second World Wars, hypnosis was used to treat post-traumatic stress. By 1955 the British Medical Association had approved hypnosis as a valid medical treatment, and the American Medical Association (AMA) followed suit in 1958. The period from 1960 onward has come to be considered as the golden age of hypnosis. As part of the humanistic movement in psychology —which could be seen as a reaction against the straitjacket of behaviorism and the old-fashioned determinism of Freudian psychoanalysis—hypnosis began to be used for many nonmedical purposes such as motivation, releasing creativity, and habit control. The idea was that if you can help people to understand themselves and reprogram their minds it would allow them to achieve their creative potential.

Making headway

Hypnosis was now considered as a possible method for treating certain psychological problems. The work of American psychiatrist and psychologist Dr. Milton Erickson and others showed that hypnosis could be developed and used in very creative ways, and was not restricted to the simple use of direct suggestion delivered in an authoritarian style.

John Butler, lecturer in medical psychology and neuroscience at King's College, London, argues that it was the failure of orthodox medicine to cure many sufferers of their psychosomatic illnesses, many of which were seen as resulting from stressful living, which provided a major stimulus to the growth in the use of hypnosis in the last 30 years. Hypnosis has been shown to be very beneficial in treating various psychosomatic illnesses.

Milton Erickson

Milton Erickson, an American psychiatrist and psychologist, is recognized as one of the most important contributors to the acceptance of both the medical use of hypnotism and the art of hypnosis. Erickson believed that even clients who are considered difficult to hypnotize can absorb new ways of thinking and learning without being aware that they are learning. He communicated by narrating stories, inventing metaphors, and recounting anecdotes. His belief was that such suggestions bypass the subject's critical faculties, and so in some instances they can avoid creating resistance.

HYPNOTISM IN WARTIME

There was an upsurge of interest in hypnosis during World War I when it was used on its own or combined with psychotherapy to help soldiers suffering from shell shock. Occasionally it was used as a battlefield analgesic. Hypnosis went into a relative decline after World War I but was studied in some psychology laboratories, notably that of Clark Hull, a respected American psychologist and the mentor of Milton Erickson. There was a revival of interest during World War II, when it was used as a treatment for post-traumatic stress, as shell shock later came to be known.

Battle hardened

Service personnel witness violent incidents as a matter of routine during wartime.

Eye Witness

In 1944, Margaret Draper, who is still alive and is now in her 70s, was working as a battlefield nurse receiving badly injured soldiers in casualty reception stations in France during World War II. She recalls that hypnosis was used routinely to treat the wounded patients when the hospital ran out of anesthetic supplies.

Devastation
On returning home, many soldiers find that they need help with stress disorders.

Disempowered
Certain types of incidents, such as the armed interrogation of a US soldier shown in this photograph, can have a long-term effect on people's psychological wellbeing.

The Modern Reputation of Hypnotism

Human plank
In the "human plank," made popular by Victorian hypnotists, muscular rigidity is suggested under hypnosis so that the subject becomes rigid enough to be supported with her head on one chair and her heels on another.

Hypnotism and mesmerism have always exerted a considerable fascination over the general public's imagination, making their practitioners' techniques a perfect vehicle for both entertainment and fiction. The tradition of the stage hypnotist goes back more than 150 years to the early nineteenth century. In the 1830s, John Elliotson, a professor of practical medicine at University College, London, invited some French mesmerists to perform a series of public demonstrations of the technique. The most famous performance was that of the quiet, reserved servant girl, Elizabeth O'Key, who was transformed into an entertaining, mischievous, mesmeric subject, regaling her audience with jokes. Victorian stage hypnotists would frequently get people in their audiences to drink ink happily, believing it to be wine.

Fictional tales

Hypnosis and mesmerism both have a strong presence in the traditional fiction of the period. In Charles Dickens's *Oliver Twist*, modern readers are often confused by the narrative descriptions of Oliver's ability to see events which are happening miles away when he is apparently asleep. Victorian readers in the late 1830s, however, would have had no difficulty in diagnosing the state into which Oliver had fallen as being "magnetic." Charles Dickens, in his turn, was to become an enthusiastic convert to the practice of mesmerism. In a similar fashion, hypnosis was associated with creative activity in a popular context in George du Maurier's famous novel *Trilby*. When she is hypnotized by the sinister character Svengali, the singer Trilby achieves a voice which is "immense in its softness, richness, and freshness."

Hypnosis has also established itself as a firm favorite with film directors. *Spellbound* (1945), starring Ingrid Bergman and Gregory Peck, depicts a psychiatrist's attempts to use hypnosis in order to retrieve a traumatic childhood memory that her patient has been suppressing. In the movie *Telefon* (1977) a hypnotist is endowed with such powers over subjects that he can get them to perform murder with just a telephone call. Then there is the enduring movie image of Dracula putting nubile young women into trance.

TRANCE AS ENTERTAINMENT

At the start of a hypnotism show, a common procedure is to select the members of the audience who will be most susceptible to hypnosis. One technique is to ask the group as a whole to clasp their hands together and then give the suggestion that it will be impossible to unclasp the hands. A few in the group will actually find that this has become the case, and thus identify themselves as good subjects. Some therapists are horrified that people permit themselves to be hypnotized in a nontherapeutic environment, objecting to the fact that there is no opportunity for a presession interview to learn what suggestions might not be good for the person, and that they may not know they have been given a posthypnotic suggestion.

Hypnotic Ability

The self-styled Russian religious leader Rasputin showed an uncanny ability to relieve the symptoms of hemophilia in Alexei, heir to the Imperial throne, making him the favorite of the Tsar and Tsarina. Some writers have suggested that Rasputin's powers were due to his skill as a hypnotist. In recent times studies have shown that hypnosis can be used to control bleeding.

Court action

The English stage hypnotist Paul McKenna was sued by Christopher Gates, a man who volunteered to take part in a performance. He danced like a ballerina, and acted as though he were a bus conductor and a lottery winner. After the hypnosis Gates claimed his personality changed and he was diagnosed as suffering from an acute schizophrenic episode. The courts ruled against Gates, saying that his mental breakdown was coincidental.

Legal Position

In the UK the 1952 Hypnotism Act allows local authorities to attach conditions to a public entertainment licence to regulate or prohibit performances of hypnotism. The Act says that you cannot hypnotize anyone under the age of 21.

Tricks of the trade

Hypnotists make members of the audience lose their inhibitions by accessing the creative areas of the brain.

The Practice of Hypnotism in Other Cultures

Druid
Practiced in pre-Christian times in Britain, Gaul, and Ireland, Druidism incorporated a form of hypnosis.

Hypnosis is represented in the philosophy and religions of many different societies across the globe. Druids called trances "magic sleep." Native Americans and some African cultures recognize the hypnotic effect of drumming and dancing, which arouses people to the point at which the conscious mind moves aside and the subconscious is exposed.

Healing

In preparation for healing, shamans have traditionally followed certain practices that allow their mental powers of concentration to be heightened. They place themselves in physical environments that are not distracting in any way, such as a completely isolated space in the forest or in a cave, and make themselves as comfortable as possible in order to descend into the "lower world." In practice, this often means visualizing an opening in the Earth, followed by a journey into that opening. The journey is frequently accompanied by drum beats, chanting, and singing. These themes of repetition and constancy allow the shaman's subconscious mind to become strongly focused on the patient in order to will a sick person to be healed.

The practice of healing by suggestion, with or without an hypnotic trance, appears to have been known to most, if not all, ancient cultures. In addition, mystics and religious saints from various cultures have described ecstatic trancelike states induced by procedures such as meditation, prayer, chanting, or particular religious rituals. The miracles of the Christian gospels appear to make much use of suggestion, and the power of belief required by the sufferer is greatly emphasized. No one school of psychology, religious belief, or philosophy, it seems, has a monopoly on the trance state. It is a universal phenomenon. A wide variety of beliefs have existed about the subject —some believed that it was caused by the gods, others that it resulted from magical powers or spirits, or simply from self-suggestion.

Mystery of Hypnotism

Throughout history an elite few have guarded the knowledge of trance, shrouding it in mysticism. As a result, it is still considered by some to be an occult science and has taken a long time to gain widespread acceptance.

WALKING ON COALS

Fire walking—the practice of walking over hot coals—is one of the oldest transformational tools known. It is practiced by Hindus, Tibetan Buddhists, and Native Americans, and is now experiencing a revival. In the US, over 30,000 people have tried fire walking to gain spiritual and emotional strength. They claim that it is a way to overcome anxiety and bolster self-esteem. Fire walkers are thought to be able to produce insensitivity to pain (analgesia) through self-hypnosis. Skeptics argue that wood coals don't conduct heat fast enough to cause critical burns, or that moisture from wet grass prevents burns.

Test of endurance
Native American shamans, whose masks represented their tribal ancestors, were called upon to walk on hot coals, rocks, or lava to purify their community.

Dislocation
Self-hypnosis allows fire walkers to dissociate vital areas of the brain from the physical messages sent from the body.

Cultural differences
There is little distinction between the creation of a trancelike state through native rituals and clinical hypnosis.

Hypnosis in the Animal World

Snake in the grass
Folklore claims that snakes hypnotize their victims to make them immobile and easy prey.

Hypnosis is by no means just a human phenomenon—over 50 species of animal are known to be susceptible to "animal hypnosis."

Animal hypnosis

Animal hypnosis refers to a curious state of immobility and partial paralysis that can be induced in animals. Chickens, for example, can be hypnotized if one seizes the bird firmly and holds it on its side on a flat surface for about 30 seconds. The chicken will struggle and then, quite suddenly, will become completely still. Other animals such as rabbits and guinea pigs can also be hypnotized if one disturbs their sense of their spatial position by suddenly putting them onto their backs.

The state of suspended animation that animals enter into to pass the winter is also considered a form of hypnotism. One theory of human hypnosis is that it is an evolutionary vestige, much like the appendix, that remains from these simple responses.

There is some evidence that individual differences in susceptibility to animal hypnosis are an inherited factor, and that through selective breeding it is possible to promote the trait.

Trout tickling

Another method of hypnotizing animals is through rhythmic stroking. Fishermen have long known the art of "tickling" trout, which has been considered a form of hypnosis. The fisherman glides his hand and arm into the pool where the fish lurks, gets his hand beneath the fish, and proceeds to stroke it with the utmost gentleness. In this way the fisherman lulls the fish into immobility, then grasps the fish in his hand and takes it out of the water.

Avoiding predators

Charles Darwin regarded animal hypnosis as "death-feigning," and today the popular explanation of animal hypnosis is that it is brought about by fear. When confronted by a threatening situation animals freeze, and thus avoid attracting attention to themselves. In some species hypnotism serves a reproductive function, making copulation safe for weak males. In the case of the spider *Dysdera erythrina*, where the female is much bigger and more powerful, the sexual courtship of the male has the power of throwing the female into an "hypnotic" state so that he can take advantage of her.

HYPNOTIC
TECHNIQUES

To experience most hypnosis techniques you will need to be guided by an expert therapist. There are, however, certain exceptions to this rule. Relaxation and visualization are both aspects of hypnosis that you can teach yourself and use productively and safely in your own home. They can be taught by experts, or learned from books and tapes. At their simplest, practicing relaxation and visualization can be regarded as a way of ensuring that you still engage in daydreams. Children undergo creative daydreaming on a regular basis. It is the natural way the mind works to offset negative states. In the past, people took advantage of gazing into the fire or going to church to free their minds from the drudgery of everyday living. Sadly, for many people the hustle and bustle of modern life has stifled this ability. All too often we forget to relax and allow our bodies to rest.

Relaxation: Overcoming the Stress Response

Relaxation

Relaxation tapes use positive language to avoid any danger of introducing negative ideas.

Regular periods of relaxation are an essential part of a person's physical and mental well-being, yet stress often prevents us from entering a naturally relaxed state. One of the persistent problems in the twenty-first century is the physiological effect that stress has on our bodies. The classic feelings of stress (dry mouth, rapid heartbeat, butterflies in the stomach) stem from the "fight-or-flight" reflex, a primitive survival response that all animals possess to get themselves out of dangerous situations.

The fight-or-flight reflex is controlled by the autonomic nervous system—the involuntary part of our nervous system that keeps us breathing and our hearts beating while we are asleep. The autonomic nervous system is divided into two parts—sympathetic and parasympathetic nerves—that have opposing effects. The sympathetic nerves increase the heart rate, while the parasympathetic nerves slow it down. When you face stress or danger, your sympathetic nervous system activity goes into overdrive, stimulating your adrenal glands (located above the kidneys) to secrete the hormone epinephrine into your blood. The result is that resources, such as the blood supply, are diverted away from your internal organs to your muscles to enable you to use them to fight or run away. When the stress is more sedentary in nature, such as impossible deadlines, exams, or relationship conflicts, and no physical action is taken, epinephrine remains in your system. The result is that the body is placed in an almost constant state of arousal, and we become depleted and panicky rather than stimulated and awake, displaying many of the physical and psychological symptoms of chronic stress.

Calming the mind

Relaxation involves the regulation of the sympathetic nervous system that controls the fight-or-flight reflex. Most methods of relaxation can be learned easily and practiced at home. They take many forms, from buying tapes containing sequences of suggestions that help you to achieve a relaxed state, to yoga and meditation. In yoga, the harmonization of breathing with yoga postures helps people to achieve a state of deep relaxation. In meditation the goal is to free the mind of its everyday clutter, by giving the brain a phrase, word, or mantra to focus on.

Big sky
To achieve the best relaxation results, visualize calming images.

RELAXATION EXERCISES
Simple breathing exercises and muscle relaxation techniques can be self-taught to reduce the physical and mental effects of stress, bringing beneficial physiological effects such as the reduction of blood pressure, the lowering of the heart rate, and generally lower levels of stress hormones. Relaxation has been shown to slow breathing, relax muscles, improve digestive processes, and increase the activity of the immune system, making the body less susceptible to illness.

Breathing Exercises

It is no coincidence that ancient traditions such as yoga and meditation both use special breathing states to achieve altered mental states. The significance of breathing is that it is involuntary, but since it can be consciously controlled, it can be used to form a bridge between the mind and the body. In the fight-or-flight response, when breathing is quick and shallow, too much carbon dioxide will be removed from the blood, prompting the classic symptoms of faintness or panic. Abdominal breathing ensures an optimum balance of oxygen and carbon dioxide in the bloodstream, helping the body to release tension.

Ancient practice
Controlled breathing techniques are a common theme in many different cultures.

Progressive Muscle Relaxation

Progressive muscle relaxation is a technique developed in the 1930s by Dr. Edmond Jacobson which aims to relax each part of your body in turn to bring a greater awareness of internal functions and increased receptivity of the senses.

Close your eyes and become aware of the weight of your body. Breathe more slowly than usual, focusing on the rhythm and the rise and fall of your abdomen. Tense the muscles in your right foot. Hold for a few seconds, then release. Go through the same process with your calf and thigh muscles. Repeat the process with your left foot and leg. Tense and relax each buttock, then your stomach muscles. Tense and relax your right fist, then the arm. Repeat with your left arm. Lift your shoulders up to your ears. Hold for a few seconds, then lower. Repeat two to three times.

Scrunch up your face, then let go and relax all of its muscles. To finish, focus on your breathing. When you are ready, wiggle your fingers and toes, gently bend your knees, and roll onto one side to get up.

Coping with stress

Learn to employ muscle relaxation techniques to help you keep your stress levels under control.

Visualization: Fulfilling Your Potential

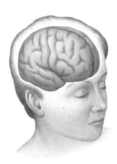

Sensory therapy

In addition to visual images you can use your sense of smell and touch to create images that motivate the mind.

Visualization is a technique that engages the imagination to help people cope with stressful situations, fulfill their potential and harness the body's natural healing processes when they are suffering from illnesses such as cancer (see pages 160–163). It is similar to dreaming, but involves deliberately engaging the conscious mind to imagine beneficial events. The practice is based on the belief that the mind and body are not separate, and that thoughts can have physical effects as well as mental ones.

People use visualization to build a place of their own inside their mind where they feel comfortable. It may be a tropical island or a sunny meadow. In times of stress, they can just close their eyes and retreat to their favorite spot on a mental vacation. The technique can also be used to practice for job interviews. It allows you to imagine yourself behaving, reacting, and looking as you would wish to in a given situation, like playing a video of the event in your head from the beginning through to a perfect outcome. Should any negative images come into your mind, you just push them away and replace them with positive ones. Sports psychologists, who train athletes, have known for some time that visualizing success increases the likelihood of it becoming a reality. Athletes are encouraged to replay over and over again in their minds mental images of an ideal performance, rehearsing and perfecting moves without the need to go around the running track or lift weights.

How to practice visualization

Find a quiet place with a comfortable chair, practice relaxation (see pages 48–51), and then once you start to feel relaxed, introduce visual imagery and suggestions. There are no rights or wrongs for the images used. It is a very subjective and personal experience.

Visualization is thought to encourage activity in the right side of the brain—the more intuitive side, which is concerned with creativity, imagination, and emotional responses. Studies have suggested that, when used with other stress reducing techniques, it can have beneficial effects on physiological processes such as breathing, heart rate, and blood pressure.

CASE STUDY: INTERVIEW

Susan, 29, had suffered a bad interview experience where she found herself feeling shaky and talking too much and too fast. Needless to say on this occasion she didn't get past the first round. She found that as she went for more senior financial consultant jobs she was interviewed by panels of four or five people, which made her feel particularly nervous. Her answers were supposed to be concise and relaxed, demonstrating that she was calm and confident in difficult situations—exactly opposite emotions to her real experience. Before her next interview Susan started reading books on interview techniques and learned about the tool of visualization, which she decided to put to the test.

Attention to detail
Susan visualized in detail how she wanted to look during the interview.

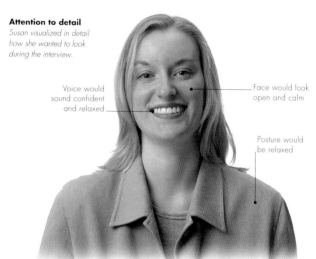

Voice would sound confident and relaxed

Face would look open and calm

Posture would be relaxed

Think Positive

TREATMENT

Susan was advised to use self-hypnosis before
entering the interview room. Just before the interview,
she visualized the feelings that she would have when she
was congratulated on getting the job. She felt a surge of
elation as positive chemicals coursed through her system.
The result was that she went into the room with feelings
of success priming her nervous system and boosting
her confidence.

RESULTS

Susan's visualization became a self-fulfilling prophecy.
She performed with intelligence and confidence. Later
that day she got a call offering her the job.

Success

*The interview followed
the same course as
Susan's visualization.*

Her face
showed quiet
confidence

Her heart
rate was
even,
relaxing
her body

Neurolinguistics: Communication Control

Programming

Experiences recreated through the five senses by our memories govern our capabilities and beliefs.

Neurolinguistic programming (NLP) is a field that was developed in the 1970s by John Grinder, a professor of linguistics, and Richard Bandler, a psychology student. Its primary aim is to understand why certain people are very effective at communicating with others, in order to help people utilize successful patterns of behavior to enhance effectiveness. Although notoriously hard to define, it

has come to be seen by its practitioners as an instruction manual for the mind. It has sometimes been described as the art and science of excellence.

What is NLP?

NLP considers that most problems in life derive from the internal models in our head. Put simply, the world we perceive is not the real world, but our own unique model that we live in as though it were real. It studies the structure of subjective experience—how each individual filters, modifies, and organizes the sensory input from the external world. As people develop a practical understanding of how their inner model works, they can learn to exchange unhelpful habits, thoughts, feelings, and beliefs for more useful ones.

At the heart of NLP is understanding how people do things well, a discipline known as modeling the structure of human excellence. NLP seeks to identify and define the thought processes and

mind patterns of top performers to
discover the difference between
competence and excellence. NLP can
be broken down into three parts.
"Neuro" refers to the neurological
processes of seeing, hearing, feeling,
smelling, and tasting, which form the
basic building blocks of experience.
"Linguistic" refers to the way we all
use language in order to represent
and organize our experience and
communicate with others. "Programming"
refers to the strategies and techniques
we use to organize these inner
processes to produce results.

Part of the development of NLP
comes from hypnosis. Bandler
observed that hypnosis is a naturally
occurring part of everyday life—we
use it to influence others, to imagine
what's going on inside someone's
head and to replay experiences in our
minds. Hypnotic methods have been
incorporated into NLP as techniques for
producing change.

THE THERAPY
SESSION

A session of hypnosis usually lasts between 30 and 60 minutes. At your first session the therapist will take a detailed history of your case, of past and current treatments, and more general matters that may be relevant to your treatment. You should mention all past events that might have a bearing on your present problems. The therapist will also deal with any concerns you may have about hypnosis. Since most people's knowledge of hypnosis owes more to fiction and folklore than reality, the therapist may need to sort out a number of misconceptions. ◌◌◌ For someone undergoing hypnosis for the first time it is only natural that they might experience some fear of the unknown, so the therapist will try to allay any anxieties. This is important, since both fear and lack of motivation can prevent the subject from fully entering the hypnotic state.

Beginning the Session: Induction

Stripped down
During a hypnosis session you will be asked to remove jewelry or contact lenses that may distract you.

The induction is the ritual that the therapist employs to achieve progressive relaxation of the body and mind and to reach a state of suggestibility known as "the trance." Many procedures are used to facilitate the patient's detachment from the awareness of his surroundings. The most usual induction is performed by the therapist talking quietly and making repeated suggestions that you are becoming increasingly relaxed and your eyelids are becoming heavy.

Other approaches include asking the client to look at a slowly turning disk, or counting slowly back from 30 to zero. As you slip into a trance you'll feel deeply relaxed. Your conscious mind will no longer control every thought as it does when you're awake. Your surroundings will become less important as you will become increasingly aware of your inner feelings and sensations. During a session your sense of time becomes distorted and you may find it hard to know for how long you have been "under."

Deepening techniques

To encourage clients to reach a deeper level of trance the therapist employs the technique of deepening. Here they will use repetitive words in phrases such as "You are going deeper and deeper, becoming more and more relaxed," and visual imagery to make you feel peaceful, such as lying in a meadow, walking, or floating in a hot air balloon on a beautiful summer's day. It is important for the therapist to have checked beforehand that the imagery is appropriate for you. If you have a fear of heights or bad hay fever, using such images could be disastrous. Patients with hay fever may find themselves reacting physically to images of a meadow as if they had actually been exposed to the allergen.

The depth of the trance refers to the degree to which someone experiences a detachment from reality and an absorption with the inner processes. It is common to speak of light, medium, and deep trances. We know that several layers of trance exist, but exactly how many there are is still an area of academic debate.

The learning curve

Going into hypnosis is a knack that has to be learned, rather like riding a bike. At first some patients can take a long time to reach even a shallow trance. But after a few sessions most people will find that the process speeds up.

GOOD SUBJECTS

Men and women seem to make equally good hypnotic subjects. It has been found generally that those who follow a highly structured career path, such as those which characterize soldiering or sailing, generally tend to find it easier to enter the trance state because they have the ability to obey orders. At the first session, the therapist will determine your susceptibility to hypnosis. There are individuals who find it particularly hard to detach themselves from the real world—these individuals are markedly resistant to hypnotic induction and achieve low scores on tests designed to measure hypnotic response.

1 *The client is asked to focus their attention on their arm, feel its weight, and let it relax until it feels detached from them. Next they are asked to imagine their arm becoming lighter and lighter.*

2 *The feeling of lightness continues until the arm has no weight at all. Finally, the client is told to let their arm go completely and to feel it floating higher and higher into the air.*

The Lemon Test

To determine whether you're a good candidate for hypnosis your therapist may perform the lemon test. Some therapists ask first-time clients to imagine looking at, feeling, picking up, and slicing a lemon in half. They must then picture themselves squeezing some of the juice into a container, smelling it, and drinking a little. Clients who are aware of salivating after the test make good candidates.

The mind pictures squeezing out and drinking lemon juice

The body responds with a physiological reaction

Suggestibility

Therapists use techniques such as hand levitation and the lemon test to discover whether clients are susceptible to suggestion. These tests are by no means infallible.

63

Trance: Getting to the Main Objective

Relaxation

Clients are more receptive to ideas when under the influence of hypnosis.

Spending time in the hypnotic state is in itself relaxing for people who spend most of their waking hours in a heightened state of arousal. It can sometimes offer welcome respite from anxiety, depression, and pain, and is similar to the mental states achieved during such disciplines as meditation and yoga. But in itself it is not considered a full psychological therapy. It is what the therapist and client do together within this state that transforms the state of hypnosis into therapy.

Correcting unhealthy patterns

With the removal of your troubles, pains, and other negative thoughts you will be able to focus on positive suggestions that the therapist makes to you. The idea is to implant constructive ideas into the subconscious mind in place of unhealthy patterns. Under hypnosis the suggestion has direct access to your subconscious, where it becomes a belief and modifies behavior or produces an effect or action.

While in a trance, subjects can be led to recognize positive abilities, be guided by the therapist to view problems from a different perspective, and gain helpful insights into past and potential future behavior. The goal is usually to get the subconscious mind to realize what the conscious mind already accepts. Visualization can also be used to enhance people's ability to achieve desired changes in their lives.

Regression hypnotherapy is used to explore the subconscious mind to locate the roots of a problem. Clients are asked to go back to an earlier time when they first experienced the feelings. The idea is to help a person come to a more positive understanding about what has happened to them. The therapist can be regarded as a teacher who is helping the individual make an adjustment in their mental and emotional life so that they can live their lives confidently and take full control over making decisions.

Ethics

Clients should never be instructed to make a particular decision regarding such things as changing their employment, or whether to marry, as the responsibility for these decisions must rest with the individual. Suggestions to undertake an immoral or illegal act, or anything that is against the client's will, should also never be made.

POSTHYPNOTIC SUGGESTIONS

Posthypnotic suggestions are delayed-action suggestions that operate on the hypnotized subject after the session and can be used to help the desired behavior the client is seeking to achieve become a reality. These usually take the form of: "When A happens, you will do B." When they are given post-hypnotic suggestions, some people have absolutely no idea why they are taking a particular course of action or thinking certain thoughts. Others will have the awareness that it has been suggested to them while in a hypnotic trance.

Enhancing performance
Performing artists such as actors and singers frequently experience a lack of confidence when appearing on stage. Their performance can be enhanced using posthypnotic suggestions that they have a real belief in their acting ability.

Weight loss

Wanting to fit into your little black dress for a special occasion can be a great incentive to lose weight. Often, however, you need more than just willpower, and posthypnotic suggestions can be used to persuade you that you have a powerful control over how much food you eat.

Giving up smoking

A helpful posthypnotic suggestion for smokers is to tell them that whenever they crave a cigarette they will drink a glass of water instead.

Ending the Session: Termination

Safety
It is the responsibility of the therapist to ensure you are orientated to the present and safe to go home.

The termination phase of hypnosis, or reawakening, signifies the end of the session, with the therapist giving clear suggestions to make the client alert. For most people the mere suggestion that they will open their eyes and be wide awake at a given cue is enough. The therapist uses a basic suggestion such as "On the count of six you will come to a fully conscious state," as well as other suggestions for awakening and experiencing wonderful feelings of well-being as they return to full awareness.

Waking up

The time taken to wake varies between different subjects. For a small minority of people it can be difficult for the therapist to arouse them. This can occur if the subject feels critical of the therapist's methods and subconsciously resists the instructions to wake up, or if they are extremely tired. There is no cause for alarm, as the sleeper will awaken after a few minutes or at most a few hours whether the hypnotist is present or not. Of its own accord the trance will turn into an ordinary sleep, from which the subject will wake in a perfectly normal manner.

Upon waking from a hypnotic trance people undergo a change in consciousness, described as the regaining of will, memory, and reasoning powers. Therapists will use their observational skills to ensure that you have no unwanted aftereffects like a hypnotic hangover, a mild headache that occasionally occurs with some clients and that is easily removed with suggestion.

After the session

The popular idea of the hypnotized person remembering nothing on waking only applies to a few people. The majority remember most of what has occurred unless the hypnotist gives them the deliberate suggestion for amnesia, but when quizzed, their recollections may prove faulty. It is not uncommon for people to complain that since they can remember much of the procedure they could not have been properly hypnotized. In such instances, the true nature of hypnosis needs to be explained to them again. There are no side effects to hypnosis other than feeling more relaxed than usual.

WHAT DOES TRANCE FEEL LIKE?

The feelings that you will experience during hypnosis are similar to dozing off to sleep. Most people feel pleasantly physically relaxed and mentally alert while they are being hypnotized. Some say it feels like meditation, others that they feel like they do after a massage, and others that it is similar to the heightened feelings induced by certain drugs. The experience of each individual under hypnosis is entirely different. Suggestions to put yourself in a relaxed state have the effect of changing muscle tension, heart rate, oxygen consumption, blood flow, and skin temperature.

Going Under

During hypnosis there is marked relaxation of physical and psychological processes. It encourages the cessation of movement, but occasional involuntary movements, such as the fluttering of the eyelids, or twitching of the fingers, can occur. The muscles relax and the pulse and breathing rates become slower as the parasympathetic nervous system (associated with involuntary movement) becomes more active than the sympathetic nervous system (associated with conscious activity). The frontal brain regions, associated with conscious reasoning, become less active.

Power of suggestion
The effect of hypnosis is to exert physiological changes throughout the body.

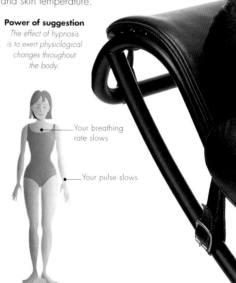

Your breathing rate slows

Your pulse slows

Under the influence
During hypnosis you will appear extremely relaxed. Occasional involuntary movements, such as fluttering of the eyelids, can occur.

Relaxation of the tear ducts: tears may appear, but not because of sad thoughts

Relaxation of the muscles: your jaw may lower and your mouth may hang slightly open

The Home Session: Self-hypnosis

Booster
Self-hypnosis empowers people to help themselves. It boosts self-confidence and reduces pain.

After a few sessions your therapist is likely to teach you self-hypnosis, which will enable you to continue the therapy at home without the aid of a therapist. This can be particularly valuable for use in treating longstanding complaints, which may require long periods of treatment before the desired changes come about. Self-hypnosis can be facilitated by your therapist using posthypnotic suggestions during treatment, such as: "You are able to hypnotize yourself by using the following trigger." A number of self-protective, posthypnotic suggestions can be included, such as: "If anyone should enter the room when you are carrying out self-hypnosis you will become instantly awake and alert."

Be warned that it can be potentially dangerous to use self-hypnosis to mask pain; pain is one of the body's warning mechanisms and this could lead to a serious illness going undetected.

Finding a routine

Patients who find self-hypnosis difficult can benefit from learning to use a self-hypnosis routine, similar to that used by the hypnotist. One method often used is to try fixing your eyes on a red spot fixed to a wall, letting your arms and legs go limp, and as your eyes become strained they will start to blink more and more until they will close by themselves. If you have any difficulty, you could ask your therapist to tape record an induction for you that contains suggestions that have been tailored specifically to you. Hypnotic induction tapes can also be purchased. It is, however, always considered best to have one or more sessions with a properly qualified hypnotist to establish suitability for the technique and to receive instruction on how to use self-hypnosis beneficially.

Setting limits

Some people fear that if they use self-hypnosis on their own they might become "stuck" in a trance. Be reassured that this isn't a realistic danger. You can set yourself a mental time limit for the end of therapy, and if you're not confident about this, use an alarm clock. If anything should happen that requires your immediate attention you would be able to sit up straight away and deal with it as you would do normally.

Survival of the fittest

An intensely competitive environment at work, together with younger colleagues eager to step into his shoes, were making Martin uptight.

CASE STUDY: STRESS

Martin, 61, had begun to find his job as a corporate lawyer in a big city firm extremely stressful. He worked in a competitive environment under the pressure of multiple deadlines and constant demands from clients to achieve success. He felt insecure, that he wasn't up to the job, and this made his work more difficult. He worked long hours and was using alcohol and cigarettes to relax. He had a few big cases coming up and felt overwhelmed by the pressure to win. His girlfriend, who had become concerned by the amount he was drinking, suggested that he should learn self-hypnosis.

Blocking it out

All too often when under stress people use alcohol, cigarettes, and recreational drugs to unwind. This does nothing to tackle the real cause of their problem.

New man
Hypnosis relieved the constant physiological state of stress occurring in Martin's body.

Tension in the neck and shoulders disappeared

Indigestion became less frequent and troublesome

Under Control

TREATMENT

Altogether Martin had four sessions of hypnosis and used it to experience feelings of deep relaxation. In the first two sessions he became confident about entering the hypnotic state and his therapist worked on bringing him deeper. In the third session he was given the posthypnotic suggestion, while under hypnosis, that if he counted back from 100 this would be his signal to achieve the self-hypnosis state. He set his alarm clock half an hour early and practiced every morning on waking. On the fourth session the therapist checked that things were going well and Martin continued self-hypnosis on a regular basis at home.

RESULTS

Once Martin started to feel more relaxed his thinking became clearer and he found he was able to achieve more at work with less effort. He felt he was no longer "running around like a headless chicken." He cut back his drinking to weekends and found that he had considerably more energy.

The Different Forms of Hypnosis

Spoiled for choice
When deciding on the form of hypnosis most appropriate for you, be led by your therapist.

There are three varieties of hypnosis: formal hypnosis (which includes relaxation and the use of suggestion); self-hypnosis; and alert hypnosis (where there is no formal relaxation component). Hypnosis itself is not a therapy, but a set of techniques that may be used to augment a particular course of treatment. Some modern forms of hypnosis are similar to psychoanalysis. The "classical" or older forms of hypnosis incorporated many different methods, including direct and indirect suggestion, and visualization.

Ericksonian hypnosis

Milton Erickson's techniques included using analogies to give suggestions outside the conscious awareness of the subject. However, direct approaches may also be used. This form of hypnosis tends not to use classical induction techniques, preferring to use strategic suggestions using the patient's daydreams and imagination.

Suggestion hypnosis

This method is often used in the treatment of addiction. The practitioner implants positive suggestions, for example that a symptom will disappear or that a pattern of behavior will change. Serious addictions also require more complex and sophisticated applications of hypnosis such as analytical hypnosis.

Analytical hypnosis

This approach—which is also known as hypnoanalysis—is a method of using hypnosis to analyze problems at a subsconscious level. It can involve regression or working through unpleasant or disturbing events from the past that have made a negative impression on the subconscious. The practitioner will regress you by asking you to recall any buried memories or emotions that might be at the root of your problem.

Cognitive-behavioral hypnosis

This uses the practical methods of cognitive-behavioral psychotherapy, a form of therapy that focuses on removing destructive or negative self-statements and patterns of behavior that are neither rational nor helpful. It helps the client to replace them with more constructive thoughts. Introducing hypnosis speeds up the whole process.

HABIT DISORDERS

Unhealthy repetitive behaviors are controlled by the subconscious rather than the conscious mind. We need to motivate the subconscious in order to overcome its resistance and permanently change a habit. Many habitual behaviors originate as neurotically determined actions that once had significance for the individual, but have now outlived the processes that created them. For example, a young person may begin to smoke as a way of signaling that they are an adult, and continue to smoke even when they mature and the assertion is no longer necessary. ⚘ Hypnosis can be used to help control destructive behavior that has become habitual to the point of compulsion, such as smoking, overeating, and alcoholism. In addition, it can be used to rein in common, irritating habits like nailbiting. ⚘ Many hypnotherapists approach such problems with ego-strengthening suggestions associated with extinction of the target behavior, such as "You feel proud and satisfied that you have broken the habit." Another treatment method, the aversion approach, emphasizes the unpleasant aspects of the behaviors.

Smoking: Kicking the Habit

The evil weed

If "cold turkey" or nicotine patches haven't worked, hypnosis may finally wean you off cigarettes.

Information from people who have been able to quit smoking successfully shows that 70 percent had made one to two previously unsuccessful attempts, 20 percent had made three to five previously unsuccessful attempts, and 9 percent had made six or more previously unsuccessful attempts before actually quitting. Nicotine is a very addictive substance and hypnosis can provide that extra helping hand.

Reasons to quit

If you are in any doubt about whether you should give up smoking, consider some of the following, albeit rather unpleasant, facts: Smoking is directly responsible for 87 percent of lung cancer cases and causes most cases of emphysema and chronic bronchitis. It is a major factor in coronary heart disease and stroke. Smoking by parents is also associated with a wide range of adverse effects in children, including asthma, increased frequency of cold and ear infections, and sudden infant death syndrome.

Within just 24 hours of stopping smoking you will experience positive benefits. Your blood pressure will be closer to normal, your pulse will drop, your hands and feet will be warmer, and you'll be at lower risk of a heart attack. Within one week of stopping, your senses of smell and taste will improve, your bronchial tubes will relax and you will be less short of breath. Within three months, your lung capacity will increase by one third, your circulation will improve, and your stamina will increase.

Calming the craving

Hypnosis can have a very powerful effect on quitting smoking after just one session. During hypnosis, the suggestions can be made that the client has no urge for a cigarette, that they find it easy to do without cigarettes, and that they do not wish to buy cigarettes.

An alternative approach, aversive conditioning, emphasizes the unpleasant aspects of the behavior: "Every time you light a cigarette you feel sick." Such techniques might also include watching videos of lung cancer operations. Clients are requested to use self-hypnosis and to repeat these ideas on a daily basis.

Different studies have shown a range of effectiveness for hypnosis in stopping people smoking, from 70 to 80 percent for a good therapist to less than 25 percent for a poor one. However, discrepancies are also caused by a variety of factors, including the level of motivation of the client.

Change for the better
A therapist can make use of a client's wish for good health by suggesting that they will feel better physically if they don't smoke.

CASE STUDY: HEAVY SMOKING

Julie, 55, was a manager of a bar and had been a heavy smoker for over forty years, having started at school to be part of the in-crowd. Her job was extremely stressful and she was finding it hard to give up her habit. She had tried everything from going cold turkey to herbal cigarettes and nicotine patches. Her problem was that at work she was continually being exposed to temptation and after a difficult day she couldn't relax without the prop of a cigarette.

Minty fresh
Julie's therapist emphasized the benefits of giving up smoking, such as her breath feeling fresher.

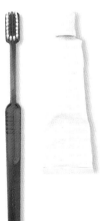

Pecuniary benefits
Another "carrot" pushed by the therapist was that she would have more money to buy herself treats.

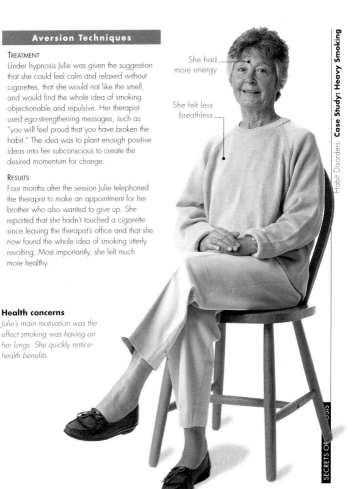

Aversion Techniques

TREATMENT

Under hypnosis Julie was given the suggestion that she could feel calm and relaxed without cigarettes, that she would not like the smell, and would find the whole idea of smoking objectionable and repulsive. Her therapist used ego-strengthening messages, such as "you will feel proud that you have broken the habit." The idea was to plant enough positive ideas into her subconscious to create the desired momentum for change.

RESULTS

Four months after the session Julie telephoned the therapist to make an appointment for her brother who also wanted to give up. She reported that she hadn't touched a cigarette since leaving the therapist's office and that she now found the whole idea of smoking utterly revolting. Most importantly, she felt much more healthy.

Health concerns

Julie's main motivation was the effect smoking was having on her lungs. She quickly notice‸ health benefits.

She had more energy

She felt less breathless

Overeating: Reducing the Craving

Counterintuitive

Hypnotic suggestions can be used to transform the taste of sweets into the taste of stinky socks.

Overeating is seen as a health problem because of its association with obesity, a problem which occurs almost exclusively in industrialized countries. Usually, a person is not considered obese unless he or she weighs 20 percent or more over the maximum desirable weight for their height. In the US, according to the Surgeon General's report on nutrition and health from 1998, up to one in four Americans are considered obese. Society's attitude toward weight often results in overweight people developing negative self-images. Obesity can also have health consequences, including the possibility of developing cancer, arthritis, varicose veins, high blood pressure, diabetes, and heart disease. While there are considerable overlaps between the problems of smoking and overeating, there is one major difference—you have to eat to live. Consequently abstinence cannot be the goal here, only a reduction in consumption.

Many people eat to reward or entertain themselves. As a child you received a candy for picking up your toys; at the movies you eat popcorn as part of the entertainment; and when you graduate from college your parents take you out for a celebratory meal. Others eat to lessen the emotional sensations of an unpleasant experience.

How hypnosis can help

Hypnosis can be used to reprogram
your subconscious attitudes to food and
give less importance to food in relation
to your feelings of well-being. It can
also be used to incorporate new
patterns of behavior in regard to
times, places, and reasons for eating.
Suggestions include that you eat only at
meal times, and that you notice when
you start to feel full and stop eating.

   Hypnosis can be used to increase
the appeal of healthy foods. It can give
suggestions to eliminate junk food
altogether, saying that unhealthy foods
are like poison to your system. It can
also be used to give specific
suggestions that you prefer skim milk to
whole milk and do not need sugar in
your tea. It can also enhance the
sensory experience of eating, with
suggestions that you should relish every
mouthful of food rather than stuffing your
face with it. The idea is to transform
yourself from a glutton into an epicure.

Junk food
Many people who put on weight exist on diets of high-fat fast food.

CASE STUDY: OVEREATING

Eric, 50, ran his own corner store. The job involved long hours serving behind the counter, and whenever he felt bored or irritable he turned to his limitless supply of sweets. He used food like a drug to lift his mood and no longer followed his body's signals of hunger. He did not have time to sit down for regular meals and survived on sandwiches and takeouts. Over five years, Eric put on 42 pounds (19 kilograms). He had tried lots of diets and lost some weight, but as soon as he stopped dieting, the weight just piled back on. He felt depressed by his inability to control his eating.

Comfort eating
The pressure of running his own business drove Eric to overeat.

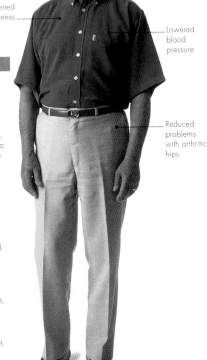

Under control

Eric found that hypnosis reorganized his thoughts about food and produced very positive results.

Resulted in better communication with his wife at mealtimes

Produced a more positive body image, increased self-esteem and control

Lessened breathlessness

Lowered blood pressure

Reduced problems with arthritic hips

Stay in Trim

TREATMENT

Under hypnosis Eric was given suggestions that he should use food to maintain his body in good health, that he would develop control over his eating, have regular meals, and feel no inclination to eat junk food. He would learn to be calm and relaxed and deal with issues and problems directly and effectively.

RESULTS

By the second session, Eric reported that he had already lost 3 pounds (1.36 kilograms), and at subsequent sessions his weight continued to drop. By the fourth session he was listening to his body's cues of hunger, planning healthy meals, and sitting down with his wife to eat dinner. The therapist felt that he was ready to continue on his own. Over the next year, while practicing self-hypnosis, Eric reached his target weight.

Abusing the Body: Habitual Behavior

You make me sick
Aversion therapy, which suggests that drinking alcohol will make the client physically ill, needs to be applied with great caution.

Nailbiting and trichotillomania (defined as the irresistible urge to pull out one's hair) often seem to be related to self-comfort, in that people have a tendency to indulge in them when they are experiencing either anxiety or a low mood. Hypnotic suggestions can be given for a temporary immobility of the arm when the limb is involved in this behavior.

Clients can also be given certain suggestions that their hair will feel terrible to touch and that they will hate to touch their hair except for grooming purposes, or that their nails will taste revolting when they are being bitten. However, therapists need to take care; if they told the hairpuller they would never touch their hair they could have problems washing it.

Alcoholism and drug abuse

Hypnosis has an important role to play in helping alcoholics and drug abusers. For starters it can be used to change their attitudes so that they actually want to get help to stop their habit.

Hypnosis can help people to recreate the feelings of well-being that they experienced under the influence of alcohol or drugs. A combination of visualization and posthypnotic suggestion can be used to allow clients to see themselves at some future event when they are offered alcohol and watch themselves refusing it and asking for a soft drink instead. This is a particularly helpful technique when they have an upcoming social event that will put their sobriety to the test.

Tics

Tics are a repeated, uncontrolled, purposeless contraction of a muscle and are often a sign of a minor psychological disorder. Since they can be made worse by stress, anxiety reduction through hypnosis can help to reduce the symptoms. Another technique is to ask the client to reproduce the tic to order during hypnosis. Then, at intervals during the course of the session, a signal that has been agreed upon in advance is given by the therapist to tell the patient to reproduce the tic. As the exercise proceeds, the patient finds it harder to produce the action to order and the involuntarily produced symptoms also decline in intensity.

PSYCHOLOGICAL
PROBLEMS

The range of psychological conditions that can be treated through hypnosis includes everything from low self-esteem to post-traumatic stress disorders. Hypnotherapy can be particularly helpful with anxiety-related conditions. Fear is a response to an immediate threat, while anxiety refers to the anticipation of an event that is less clearly defined. ❧ The symptoms people experience during panic attacks are a natural part of the body's fight-or-flight response, which provides a surge of energy to fight an attacker or to run away. The body tenses, producing the classic symptoms of a fast heartbeat, shortness of breath, and butterflies in the stomach. As the body becomes sensitized one may begin to anticipate panic attacks, avoiding situations that might provoke them. Ultimately one avoids any situation, person, or object that might evoke feelings of arousal or anxiety.

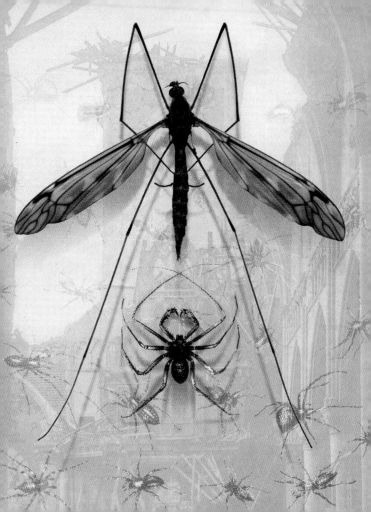

Confidence Problems: Boosting the Ego

That sinking feeling
People who suffer from low self-esteem may find that it affects many areas of their lives.

Problems of low self-esteem, which on the face of it may seem quite minor, can blight people's lives and make them lose out on major opportunities. They may lack the confidence to attend social functions, or to talk to the opposite sex, and may be held back at work. An extreme example is the condition known as social phobia, in which people go out of their way to avoid social gatherings. When they are forced to mix with people they suffer from the panic attack symptoms such as palpitations, sweating, dry mouth, and blushing. It is a problem worth tackling, since social phobics are around nineteen times more likely to abuse alcohol and drugs than others.

Minor problems

Under hypnosis people can be programmed with suggestions that make them feel good about themselves: that they feel calm, confident, and actually enjoy socializing. They are taught not to undermine themselves with negative thoughts. To shine at a particular occasion, such as a party or job interview, people can be hypnotized and then visualize the event, repeating to themselves that they feel comfortable and calm, and that they feel at ease with the world. These feelings will then reemerge when they are in the actual situation. Self-hypnosis can thus develop a person's confidence in the particular situation in which they feel limited. Trigger words can be used to change the way they feel about a situation. Physical symptoms such as blushing, sweating, or trembling can be helped through hypnosis, by exposing clients to the feared event through visualization, and then gradually acclimatizing them to the situation.

Deeper problems

Most people lacking confidence are likely to improve under the power of hypnotic suggestion. There are, however, those who have deeper problems that need to be tackled at a more fundamental level. They may have feelings of low self-esteem because they were undermined as a child or perhaps beaten or sexually abused. Others may have deep-rooted feelings to do with parents or authority figures who made them feel insecure, unwanted, or a failure. In many of these cases, hypnoanalytical work such as regression therapy (see pages 100–101) is needed.

Invisibility
Lack of confidence can lead some people to shut themselves away from society altogether.

CASE STUDY: CONFIDENCE

Mark, a 30-year-old radio journalist, found that his feelings of self-doubt were making his job difficult and making it hard to communicate with women. Whenever he was with people, either at work or in a social situation, he found that he had negative thoughts running through his head that he "wasn't good enough" and that people "didn't like" him. Inevitably, this became a self-fulfilling prophecy. A new relationship with a woman whom he really liked was not developing as he had hoped. He felt that his negative attitudes were crippling his life. A visit to a stage hypnotist show made him think that hypnotic suggestions might help.

Vulnerable
Mark's lack of confidence stemmed from his mother, who didn't help him to build a belief in himself as a child.

Gaining Confidence

TREATMENT

Under hypnosis, Mark was given direct suggestions that he felt confident with people, liked socializing, felt confident in his work and altogether good about himself. He visualized himself at a social function where he was chatting with people he had met for the first time with confidence and charm. The treatment was emphasized with a tape containing suggestions for confidence that he played to himself at home while practicing self-hypnosis.

RESULTS

After five sessions of hypnosis Mark noticed a major change in his attitude to life. He started to feel more confident about his work, and more assertive in dealing with colleagues and interviewees. He felt he was being more creative in writing his scripts. His relationship with his girlfriend flourished—she found him easier to be with and they had decided to rent an apartment together.

He no longer blushed when introduced to people

His hands no longer trembled in confrontational situations

Strength
Hypnosis helped Mark to lose his negative self-image and communicate with others with increased confidence.

Phobias: Dealing with Fear

Creepy crawly

Arachnophobia—fear of spiders —may be rooted in a fear of poisonous creatures that has stayed with us since primitive times.

A phobia is a persistent, irrational fear of, and desire to avoid, a particular object or situation. You are not born with a phobia—it is a learned response. Common phobias include claustrophobia (fear of enclosed spaces), agoraphobia (fear of open spaces), and acrophobia (fear of heights). There are many altogether weirder phobias such as selenophobia (fear of the moon), pogonophobia (fear of beards), and triskadekaphobia (fear of the number 13). Phobias can exist in the lives of people who may be otherwise reasonably well adjusted. Sufferers often recognize their fears to be unrealistic, but still feel unable to confront them. To complicate the situation further, people may have a phobia about one thing when the underlying fear relates to something entirely different. Typically, an anxiety builds up and the person attaches it to something in their environment. For example, the person who dislikes their job may develop a fear of buses, because the bus is the only means they have of getting to work.

People with phobias can experience a fear so intense and debilitating that it begins to affect the way they live their lives. Confronted with the phobic situation they experience the classic symptoms of panic attacks such as sweating, trembling, feeling faint, and may even feel as though they are dying. The results are a loss of any confidence and feelings of self-worth, and increasing frustration as they feed energy into unwanted emotions. When phobias start to interfere with day-to-day functions in a person's emotional, social, or work life, they need treatment.

Desensitization

Desensitization behavior therapy, where a situation is created in which the client is slowly and by stages brought into contact with their fear, is a popular therapy for phobias, but can be very traumatic. Hypnosis can be used to provide a gentler option. In confrontation inductions, phobics are asked to imagine themselves face to face with fear itself. They are then asked to notice how weak the fear appears and told that they feel completely at ease in its presence. Regression (see pages 100–101) is used to identify the cause of a phobia that is rooted in the client's past.

Family ties
His job in a New York restaurant meant that Theodosis had to fly back to Greece when he wanted to visit his family.

CASE STUDY: FEAR OF FLYING

Theodosis, 25, was a Greek waiter working in a New York restaurant who needed to fly home to visit his family in Athens. He wanted to see his sister's new baby and attend his grandmother's eightieth birthday celebrations. His problem was that he had developed a severe phobia about flying that made the trip seem impossible. His last flight had been unusually turbulent and the woman sitting next to him had become extremely anxious. It was as if her fears had transmitted themselves to him. Now whenever he thought about flying, he started to sweat and tremble.

Fear
For people with a plane phobia the very thought of flying can be enough to trigger a panic attack.

Fearful thought patterns were dispelled

Calming of fears eased symptoms of panic attack such as fast heart rate

Resolved.

Hypnosis reprogrammed Theodosis's feelings about flying, associating the experience with calm and relaxation.

Flying High

TREATMENT

At the first session, Theodosis was put into a trance and the therapist told him to imagine that he was traveling in a car to the airfield. In the next session he was told to visualize himself getting onto the plane and in the final session he visualized himself taking a short flight around the airfield. During all the sessions, the therapist implanted positive suggestions that he would feel relaxed during the flight and wouldn't suffer from any feelings of anxiety.

RESULTS

Nine months later, after just three sessions of treatment, Theodosis phoned the therapist and told him that he had successfully made the trip back to Greece. In fact, he had found the trip so pleasurable that he announced that he was now thinking of applying for a job as an airline flight attendant.

Buried Trauma: Healing with Regression

Going back
During age regression you relive your past, not as a memory but as though you were there experiencing the event again.

Regression therapy enables the client to reevaluate events in their past and gain a better perspective on them. It can ease the emotional response to certain traumatic childhood events that occurred when the client may not have been old enough to understand their significance. One danger therapists need to be aware of, however, is that in examining the origins of a problem they may bring others to the surface that must also be dealt with. Therapists use their clinical intuition to decide when regression is appropriate. The technique involves taking clients back by saying "You are now going back, getting smaller and younger, going back into your past." Before entering hypnosis, you may be asked to decide how best to protect yourself if necessary—this might be with an imaginary weapon.

Age regression is commonly used to identify which particular factor caused a phobia. The client lets their minds drift back and sees themself at the age when they first experienced the phobia. Once people are helped to realizewhat it was that caused the phobia, the next step is to let go of the old emotional tie to that memory. One technique is to ask them to imagine the incident on a movie screen and then see themselves coping effectively, cutting the cord to free themselves from the negative event. Regression can also help clients who are feeling low to remember how contented they felt a few years back, and help them to believe that they can regain these feelings.

Child abuse

In cases of child abuse, regression can have tremendous value because it motivates recall of childhood memories and traumas, which can then be dealt with. Once the scenes and situations are made available, the client can begin to understand them and sever emotional ties with them.

People vary in their ability to recall events and there is currently much debate about false memory syndrome, in which false ideas can be implanted. Here, people vividly imagine events that they swear have happened. It is important for clients to realize that the events they recall during hypnosis may not be the actual truth. But at the same time, if they think it is true, the therapist can work with it.

Satiated desires
Many people experiencing psychological conflicts take refuge in food.

CASE STUDY: CHILD ABUSE

Helen, a 28-year-old secretary, had recently become engaged. This brought to the surface memories of childhood abuse by her father that she had managed to suppress. She found it difficult to trust any man and began to feel hostility toward her fiancé. She had put a block on the physical side of the relationship and had avoided the problem by saying that she wanted to wait until they were married. Her feelings of frustrated anger turned into feelings of depression. Since her father had died when she was a teenager she was unable to confront him with these issues or to discuss them with her mother. She sought refuge in food and started putting on weight.

Shattered
All too often when children are abused by a trusted adult they feel that they are somehow responsible for the abusive actions.

Regaining Trust

TREATMENT

The therapist used regression to return to the traumatic events of Helen's childhood, about which she had only vague memories. It showed her that her father no longer had any power over her. It allowed her to see him as the weak, warped person that he was and impressed upon her that the abuse was not her fault. Through hypnosis the therapist made Helen understand at a subconscious level that the past was over, that she was in control of her own destiny, and that she could now get on with leading her own life.

RESULTS

At the fourth session Helen reported that she felt as though a tremendous burden had been lifted. She felt as though healing was going on in her body, and that she was beginning the process of forgiving her father. She no longer experienced feelings of anger toward her fiancé, felt much more relaxed when she was alone with him, and didn't have any uncomfortable feelings about touching or cuddling him. At work her productivity had gone up, and she felt happy and confident enough to start making plans for her wedding.

Mental turmoil eased, making Helen's thoughts clearer
A healthy diet led to better digestion

Back on track

One effect of Helen's hypnotherapy was that she stopped eating junk food, and returned to a healthy weight in time for her wedding.

Reincarnation: Past Life Regression

A previous life
Can looking back in time identify events that are draining emotional energy in your present life?

Past life regression involves going back to former lives under the influence of hypnosis. This is thought to provide evidence for reincarnation, but some therapists view it as the mind's way of symbolizing buried thoughts and emotions. Believers in reincarnation say that your present life is a composite of everything you have ever felt or experienced in former lives, and that unresolved issues from former lives result in physical tension, strong emotions or fears, or habitual thoughts or gestures that absorb energy. Occasionally, the technique is used for clients who have not progressed through regression to childhood.

Time travel

The method used is an extension of normal regression. The therapist takes you back through this lifetime, to your childhood, to the womb, to an astral plane looking down on the world, back further to a time and place where you were a different person in a different body. Subjects are asked about significant past events, and may recall times and places of which they have no conscious knowledge.

Many believe that this is cryptoamnesia—in which the subject embroiders a fantasy, probably about an event they have read about and forgotten. Whatever their source, recall of the events can have therapeutic effects, and may resolve emotional or nervous complaints.

Virginia Tighe

In the 1950s, the book *The Quest for Bridey Murphy* by Morey Bernstein was published. It recounted the experiences of Virginia Tighe who, when hypnotized, spoke with an Irish accent, danced a jig, and said that her name was Bridey Murphy and that she lived in nineteenth-century Ireland. Later it was discovered that Tighe had been recounting tales told to her by a woman who had been brought up in Ireland.

Like Virginia Tighe, in 95 percent of cases past life memories can be accounted for. Under hypnosis people have been regressed again and asked where they obtained the information—often the ideas have come from a book or other source. However, around 5 percent of cases remain unexplained.

Again and again
Some hypnotists believe that each life you live offers an opportunity to learn more spiritual lessons.

REINCARNATION

Over 20 years, Arnall Bloxham, a distinguished hypnotherapist from Cardiff, tape-recorded 400 examples of reincarnation. The most renowned of these is the case of a Welsh woman who used the pseudonym Jane Evans, and described in detail six previous lives: as the wife of a tutor in Roman times; as a Jewess in twelfth-century York; as a serving girl to a French medieval merchant prince; as a maid of honor to Catherine of Aragon; as a poor seamstress in London in Queen Anne's time; and finally as a nun in an American convent in Maryland at the beginning of the twentieth century.

Fantasy
Finding a glamorous former existence can provide compensation for a life that has grown mundane.

Pogrom at York

REBECCA

The recording of Rebecca, the Jewess in twelfth-century York, describes harrowing violence, fire, and the death of Rebecca and her daughter. She describes the racial tensions in York that led up to the massacre by fire of the city's Jewish population at Clifford's Tower, and her escape, after which she took shelter in the crypt of a small church outside the city gates with her daughter. She describes hearing soldiers entering, her terror that they were about to be discovered, then darkness.

FURTHER INVESTIGATION

In his book *More Lives Than One*, written in 1976, Jeffrey Iversen investigated claims made by Rebecca and some of Bloxham's other subjects. He visited places where the regressions were set, cross-checked details against known or presumed historical fact and interviewed historians. One such historian, Professor Barrie Dobson from the University of York, found much of the detail of Rebecca's story "impressively accurate." Professor Dobson felt that St. Mary's in Castlegate, York, matched the description of the church Rebecca took shelter in. But the church did not have a crypt. Six months later, however, a workman discovered what may have been a crypt, a structure which dated back to the Romanesque period (before 1190).

This discovery gave credibility to Rebecca's story. Significantly, her version of events of the massacre was not a straightforward rewording of the history books. She revealed things that could not have been gleaned from books or stories. Iversen concluded that her knowledge defied rational explanation, but other researchers are more skeptical and claim that there are some inaccuracies in the memories unearthed in this case.

Ordeal by fire
Jane Evans's account of the massacre of York's Jewish population agreed with the known historical detail.

Depression: Lifting the Clouds

Destined for depression?
Clinical depression affects about 10 percent of men and 20 percent of women at some time in their life.

The word depression covers a wide range of mental states, from passing moods of negativity to clinical depression, a major health disorder characterized by a persistent and abnormal lowering of mood and a loss of interest in usual activities. Doctors make a diagnosis of clinical depression when a person suffers from a group of symptoms for longer than two weeks.

The symptoms include despair, bouts of uncontrollable weeping, lethargy, self-hatred, exhaustion, hypochondria, and in extreme cases, delusions and hallucinations.

Clinical depression is a common emotional disorder. Aside from the biological causes of depression (which are generally treated with drugs to raise levels of neurotransmitters), depression can occur as a result of events that happen in a person's life and their attitude toward them. For example, it is common for people to become depressed when they lose their job or experience bereavement.

Rebuilding the ego

While the use of hypnosis cannot perform miracles, it can help some people to accept their situation and to no longer feel angry about the event. In some cases, hypnosis may be used in conjunction with behavioral and cognitive therapy.

The process of hypnosis used purely as a means of relaxation may help some depressed people. It can also be used to resolve traumatic memories and to seek out the roots of people's feelings of inadequacy (see pages 100–101). Ego-strengthening inductions can be tailored to the needs and characteristics of individual patients to make them feel good about themselves. But since the technique is used to amplify positive feelings, there must be some positive feelings present in the first place for it to have any effect. Hypnosis requires the active participation of the patient, and can be difficult if a depressed patient is experiencing feelings of hopelessness, a lack of energy, and an inability to get involved in anything.

The Clenched Fist

In this technique, good feelings are anchored to the right hand and bad ones to the left. The left fist is clenched to dispel negativity, and the right, when clenched, prompts positive thoughts.

Dead of night
*Isolation and the lack of
distractions at night can lead
to black thoughts, nightmares,
and panic attacks.*

CASE STUDY: DEPRESSION

Edward, 65, had recently retired from a job in journalism on a national newspaper. Having been used to a stimulating and demanding career, he was now finding it difficult to find his new direction in life and manage his free time. He also felt that he had failed to fulfill some of his potential, having never made it to the top of his profession. He experienced a crisis about the lack of meaning in his life. His children had moved away from home, leaving him with few responsibilities. He began to feel that there was not much to look forward to. One night he had a panic attack during which he experienced an intense fear of death. He began suffering from early morning insomnia and profoundly negative thoughts and feelings.

On the job
*Edward derived most
of his feelings of
self-worth from his
status as a journalist.*

Regaining Confidence

TREATMENT

Edward's treatment involved a combination of hypnopsychotherapy and straightforward hypnotism. The hypnopsychotherapy involved counseling about his belief system and his view of himself in life. In hypnosis he was given suggestions that he would feel more positive and confident about his future, and that he had many more productive years left in which he could be creative with his skill as a writer. He was also given suggestions to help him feel good about himself.

RESULTS

After six or seven sessions Edward began to show a big improvement in his outlook. The cloud of depression lifted and he felt more positive and assertive about his future. The intense feelings of anxiety eased. Once again he began to feel in control and confident enough to take on some freelance journalistic assignments.

Recovery
Edward's negative feelings dissolved when hypnosis reprogrammed his thought structure and recovered his enthusiasm for life.

Ego-strengthening inductions reminded him of his abilities

He started writing again

Post-traumatic Stress: Healing Anguish

Long-standing effect
Traumatic events can leave scars on the mind as well as the physical body.

Post-traumatic stress disorder (PTSD) is a specific form of anxiety that comes on after a stressful or frightening event. The trigger can be a man-made event or a natural disaster involving violence or serious injury. The idea that intense stress can leave sufferers traumatized for long periods first emerged during World War I. Doctors attributed "hysterical" symptoms to the pressure caused by exploding shells. During World War II, psychiatrists recognized that shell shock had its roots in the mind rather than in the physical body, and so they renamed the condition "combat neurosis."

Today, post-traumatic stress disorder is recognized not just as a phenomenon of battle, but as a mental disorder that can follow any disaster or traumatic event. It affects surviving victims and bystanders alike.

The legacy of trauma

Following a traumatic event, some survivors develop overwhelming feelings of intense fear, terror, and helplessness. Symptoms include intrusive and unwanted thoughts and memories in which their minds flash back to the event, hallucinations and nightmares, disorientation, a sense of personal isolation, and disturbed sleep and concentration. It is as if their minds are replaying the event and attempting to understand it more fully and from different perspectives. They can also experience "survivor guilt" because they survived the disaster while others died. The disorder can create many problems in relationships at work and at home, because sufferers become withdrawn and cannot concentrate on the events of the present.

Reprogramming

Hypnosis can be used to help people look again at what has happened and to reprogram their minds to reduce anxiety and stress and gain a greater understanding of their symptoms and an acceptance of the traumatic event. Hypnosis is used for mental and physical relaxation, the reduction of disturbances of thoughts and feelings, and for learning to function more effectively again. It gives the sufferer closure, puts them back in control, and helps them to move away from their feelings of being a victim.

Preoccupied

Those who are suffering from post-traumatic stress disorder may find themselves unable to cope with work and family.

PTSD: CASE STUDY

Emma, a 32-year-old hairdresser, was involved in a major rail disaster. She was uninjured but saw many distressing scenes. At first she experienced profound shock, but after a few days she began to feel a little better. Suddenly, two weeks later, she started having graphic flashbacks in which she relived the event in intense detail. These happened both when she was asleep and when she was awake. They came to dominate her life to such an extent that she felt she couldn't concentrate on anything else and stopped going to work. She became withdrawn from her husband and friends, who she felt had no idea what she was going through. Her husband felt that her character had changed overnight, and had no idea how to help.

Survivors

Those who have been involved in major disasters and escaped unscathed may have feelings of guilt.

Letting Go

TREATMENT

Emma's therapy started with counseling
sessions in which she was asked to describe
exactly what happened during the traumatic
incident. In the third session she was regressed
to the event using hypnosis to help her to see
how her mind had become stuck in the
experience, and that she could begin the
process of letting go and starting to move on.
It was in her past and need not affect her
future. Hypnosis was also used to help
achieve relaxation and to give her ego-
strengthening messages to improve her
self-confidence.

RESULTS

Over four months of regular therapy, Emma's
nightmares became less intrusive and she
started to feel more relaxed during the day.
She got to the point where she could last
whole mornings without thinking about the
event, and eventually whole days. Her
concentration returned and she felt able to
think about other things and even commute
to work on the train. She started to
socialize with friends and talk more
openly about her feelings to her husband.

The nightmares slowly
receded and powers of
concentration returned

Tension in the
physical body
began to ease

The feelings
of isolation
lessened and
relationships healed

Open up

*Emma began to open up
to her husband as a result
of intensive hypnosis, which
helped her to move forward
in her life again.*

Sexual Problems: Restoring the Libido

Anxiety
Hypnosis can help to remove feelings of awkwardness and the fear of poor sexual performance.

Sexual problems can be defined as an inability to derive pleasure and satisfaction from sexual activity. The cause of the problems may be physical or psychological. One of the main barriers to successful performance and enjoyment is simply anxiety. Worrying about performance can cause impotence or premature ejaculation. Repeated failure during intercourse leads to anxiety, frustration, and apprehension. Groin muscles need to relax to allow blood to flow into the penis and maintain an erection. Anxiety blocks the flow of blood into the penis and prevents the erection. Self-hypnosis will help men to relax. Visualization can be employed to help direct blood flow to the penis. Ego-strengthening messages can be given during hypnosis to boost their performance.

Problems for women

In women, unconscious conflicts concerning sexual activity may reveal themselves in the condition vaginismus. This is an involuntary reflexive spasm of the muscles of the vagina and perineum that prevents penetration from taking place. The causes are thought to include the fear of pain during intercourse and negative attitudes toward the body or the act of sex. Hypnosis can help women to relax, and regression therapy can be employed to reveal the cause of the problem and then resolve it.

Satisfying sex

Hypnosis can help people's sexual
performance in many other ways.
People who feel guilty about enjoying
sex can be given suggestions that they
can relax and let go. For people who
feel that they have just lost interest in
sex, age regression can be used to
recall pictured memories of satisfying
sexual activity. Visualization can be
used to help people respond to their
partner in the way they want to. Just as
visualization might prepare someone for
a job interview, it can prepare them for
a sexual encounter. If people feel self-
conscious about their bodies they can
be given suggestions that their body is
perfectly attractive.

Infertility

Hypnosis may also help some couples
to conceive. There are theories that
stress can prevent conception, and
since hypnosis can decrease the effects
of stress, it may help.

MEDICAL PROBLEMS

Hypnosis is often used to complement conventional medical treatments for many conditions. It can help to overcome the pain of headaches, childbirth, cancer, and severe burns. In the operating theater surgeons are allowing hypnosis to be introduced to lessen anxiety, reduce bleeding, and cut down on the amount of anesthesia needed. In certain cases it has been used for drug-free surgery. For people with serious illnesses, such as cancer or AIDS, it may be used to stimulate the immune system. One of the most common uses of hypnosis is to treat psychosomatic illnesses to which factors such as stress are believed to contribute. Examples include some cases of asthma, eczema, and irritable bowel syndrome.

High Blood Pressure: Relaxing the Arteries

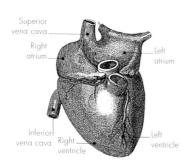

Superior vena cava
Right atrium
Left atrium
Inferior vena cava
Right ventricle
Left ventricle

Central muscle
The contraction of the heart is responsible for blood pressure.

During each heartbeat, the heart muscle contracts to push blood around the body. The pressure produced by the heart is at its highest when the muscle contracts, and is known as the systolic pressure. The heart muscle relaxes before the next contraction and the pressure falls to its lowest, known as the diastolic pressure. Each type of pressure is expressed in millimeters of mercury (mmHg). People are generally considered to have high blood pressure if they have a systolic pressure above 160 mmHg and a diastolic pressure above 90 mmHg. Blood vessels tend to be less elastic in older people, making their blood pressure higher.

Hypertension

High blood pressure, or hypertension, is extremely common, affecting 10 to 20 percent of the population. In 90 percent of people the cause remains a mystery. Risk factors include being overweight, unfit, drinking large amounts of alcohol, and stress.

In stressful situations, the heart rate increases and blood pressure rises. A well known example is "white coat hypertension" in which a patient's blood pressure rises simply as a result of having it measured by a doctor. When these people measure their pressure at home they sometimes discover that it is normal.

Although the effects of short-term stress on blood pressure are well documented, the role chronic stress plays in the formation of chronic hypertension is less certain. It is unclear whether hypnosis alone is enough to control certain chronic blood pressure problems.

Nevertheless many therapists will offer hypnosis for hypertension. In addition to relaxation under hypnosis, another popular method is getting clients to visualize the psychosomatic processes involved in an attempt to modify the physical response. Clients can be asked to visualize their arteries softening and becoming more elastic, allowing the pressure of blood flowing through them to be reduced.

Practical Tip

In some cases the therapist will monitor the client's blood pressure in order to shape imagery and the suggestions used.

Anxiety
Just being in a medical setting is enough to raise some people's blood pressure.

CASE STUDY: HYPERTENSION

Joan, aged 60, had suffered from borderline high blood pressure for ten years. Her doctor found that it had risen and added a thiazide diuretic drug to the beta blockers that she was already taking. The condition was exacerbated by her personality; she was a high achiever who had run her own business. Now retired, she was continually on the go, and could be impatient and aggressive. This was compounded by her husband's easy-going character; he had a mild manner, and tended to get taken advantage of by other people. The doctor recommended that Joan try hypnosis to help her to relax.

Put your feet up
Taking time out and relaxing can have a major impact on reducing blood pressure.

SOOTHING CUP OF TEA

BLOOD PRESSURE MONITOR

Feelings of
agitation lessened
and relaxation
became easier

Intake of anti-
hypertensive drugs
lowered with the
agreement of a doctor

The risks of
stroke and
heart attack
were lowered

Relaxation

TREATMENT

Although the effects of short-term stress on blood pressure are well documented, whether chronic stress can be responsible for chronic hypertension is still a matter of debate. Nevertheless, many therapists offer hypnosis for hypertension. In this case, the therapist used the state of hypnosis to help Joan relax. He also used suggestions that would help her to feel relaxed in her everyday life. She also visualized her arteries becoming more relaxed and her blood flowing more easily. She took home a self-hypnosis tape that had been specially made for her, and practiced religiously. Altogether she attended four sessions.

RESULTS

After the first session Joan's blood pressure fell dramatically. It returned to a milder level, and her GP decided that she could do without the thiazide diuretic.

Persistence

Joan's determination to stick to her program of self-hypnosis maintained the beneficial effects of the hypnotherapy sessions.

Eczema: Stress-calming and Invisible Anesthesia

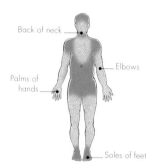

Common sites

Eczema starts with tiny blisters, then enters the weeping stage, becomes encrusted, and may lead to thickened skin.

- Back of neck
- Elbows
- Palms of hands
- Soles of feet

Eczema is an inflammation of the skin that usually causes itching and is sometimes accompanied by scaling or blisters. Eczema can be divided into "contact" or "allergic" conditions. Contact eczema is triggered by an environmental irritant, such as a chemical; allergic eczema results from a hypersensitive immune system over-reacting to something—house-dust mites, for example, which most people find harmless. Seborrheic eczema, in which red, flaky patches develop on the face and scalp, tends to occur in areas where the sebaceous glands are numerous, and is caused by overproduction of the skin's natural oils.

The effects of stress

Many sufferers report that stress appears to exacerbate their condition. Whether or not this is actually the case is unknown, since it is hard for doctors to judge whether the stress predated the eczema or was subsequently caused by the eczema. The timing of the stress is largely academic, however, because the important fact is that it exists, and hypnosis and relaxation have an important role to play in reducing a person's tendency to scratch, and alleviating their anxiety. Many eczema patients are children and they can find it very difficult to control their urge to scratch the affected areas. For this reason hypnosis may have a particularly helpful role to play in childhood atopic eczema.

Relieving the itching

Under hypnosis, direct suggestions can be made to reduce the symptoms of itching, anxiety, and insomnia. The suggestion can be made that as soon as the patient's nails touch their skin they will become aware and stop scratching, even if they are asleep. Relief of itching is one of the most important eczema treatments, as it breaks the itch–scratch cycle.

Patients can be trained to produce local anesthesia in an area so that they feel no need to scratch. One method is to visualize the application of cool water to relieve the itching, and to then associate that sensation with the touch of the hand. The patient practices placing a hand over the itch and feels the same soothing and relief as they would from water.

Irritation
Hand eczema is usually the result of irritation caused by substances such as detergents. It is exacerbated by stress.

CASE STUDY: ECZEMA

Paul, aged 26, started suffering from eczema as a teenager. He found that his skin problems always got worse around exam time when he was under particular stress. He now had a job as a realtor, where he was finding that the pressure to perform at work made him feel stressed. He suffered from raised scaly patches on his arms and legs, which started to itch very badly. When he was under stress he got into the habit of picking at the patches, which only made the itching worse.

Off guard
Relaxing situations, like being in bed at night, can be prime times for scratching.

TREATMENT

Paul had five sessions of hypnosis using direct
suggestion to reduce the itching. He was told
that his skin would feel wonderfully cool and
comfortable. On the third session he was
given a self-hypnosis tape, which he practiced
when he was in bed at night—a prime time
for scratching.

RESULTS

Almost immediately Paul started to respond
to the suggestions and soon felt that he was
gaining the upper hand. Over the weeks
of treatment the red patches got
progressively smaller and less
raised and irritated. By the end
of the sessions his skin was
virtually back to normal.
Having the hypnosis tape
gave him the confidence that
if the skin condition ever
returned he would be able to
get it under control. Treating
his skin problems had an
additional effect of helping
his performance at work and
making him feel less anxious.

Resolving stress
encouraged more
effectiveness
at work

Hypnotic suggestion
cooled patches of
inflamed skin,
allowing them to heal

Self-confidence

*Feeling less self-conscious
about his skin made Paul more
outgoing and better able to
deal with clients at work.*

Medical Problems **Case Study: Eczema**

SECRETS OF HYPNOSIS

127

Asthma: Prevention Through Imagery

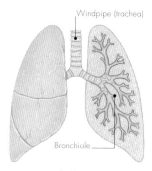

Windpipe (trachea)

Bronchiole

The lungs

Air travels down the windpipe into the main bronchi, the bronchioles, and finally the alveoli, where gas and blood are exchanged.

Asthma is a condition in which the airways in the lung become inflamed and are sensitive to specific triggers that cause them to narrow, reducing the amount of oxygen reaching the lungs and resulting in coughing, and shortness of breath. Triggers include pollen, exercise, or house-dust mites. It is one of the most common chronic diseases, affecting around 7 percent of the population. Studies have shown a four-fold increase in the number of children suffering from asthma over the last 20 years, but the reasons for this are debatable.

The effects of stress

While stress does not cause asthma, psychological factors can exacerbate the condition. Strong emotions like anger, stress, or joy can trigger an attack. Older children and adults sometimes find that their asthma gets worse at times of stress, such as during an argument. Suffering a severe asthma attack is, in itself, very stressful. When an attack occurs, hyperventilation is accompanied by anxiety, which aggravates the breathing problems, which can result in a vicious cycle of escalating symptoms.

It should be noted that hypnosis is a preventative treatment and should not be used in an acute attack in which life-saving medications must be employed.

Hypnosis has a role in promoting general relaxation, and in the exploration of underlying anxieties, which are known to exacerbate the condition. Relaxation can reduce the incidence and severity of asthmatic episodes, and self-hypnosis can alleviate asthma at the start of an attack. Here, visual imaging of the expansion of the airways can be used. Hypnosis is not appropriate, however, when someone is in the throes of an attack. To suggest to an asthmatic patient that she is not wheezing during an attack would reduce respiratory drive and endanger breathing.

Medical studies have demonstrated the benefits of hypnosis in lessening the occurrence of asthma attacks. A year-long study of 16 asthmatic patients who were taught self-hypnosis showed that their admissions to hospital were reduced from 44 in the year before starting therapy to 13 in the year after (Morrison, 1988).

Lifesaver
Finding themselves without their inhaler produces enough anxiety to trigger an attack in some asthma sufferers.

CASE STUDY: ASTHMA

Laura, a 30-year-old nurse, wanted to gain control over her asthma attacks. Her symptoms went back to childhood, and she found that whenever she became tired, stressed, or emotional, this triggered an attack. She had recently been through a divorce and was facing the fact that she had problems in her life, such as feelings of low self-esteem, that were not going to go away. She was afraid that no one else would find her attractive. The stress had also made her symptoms worse. She had suffered a few instances when she had felt totally unable to breathe and had thought about going to the hospital. Attending a course on hypnosis as part of her work made her realize that it might help bring her symptoms under control.

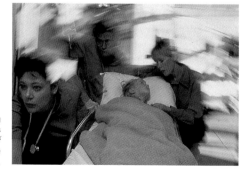

Gasping
Some asthma patients like Laura live in fear of a severe attack which could hospitalize them.

TREATMENT

Laura had six sessions of hypnosis. In treatment she was given suggestions that her breathing would feel calm and relaxed. The aim was that whenever she thought about breathing she would associate it with feelings of calm. Her therapy also included suggestions about self-love and self-respect to boost her self-esteem.

RESULTS

By the second session, Laura was really starting to feel better. As the sessions continued she found that she was having progressively fewer attacks in the intervals between them. She reached the point where her asthma had virtually stopped and she was not using any preventative medication.

Laura began to take more interest in her appearance

The lessening of symptoms led her to begin attending a gym to get fit

Her eating habits were brought under control and she began to lose weight

Domino effect

Defeating one problem helped to boost Laura's self-esteem, and brought benefits to the other aspects of her life.

Irritable Bowel: Breaking the Anxiety Cycle

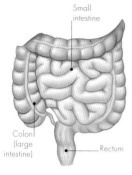

Small intestine

Colon (large intestine)

Rectum

The intestines

The intestines form a long tube divided into two main sections, the small intestine and the large intestine.

Symptoms of irritable bowel syndrome (IBS) include abdominal pain, cramping, bloating, and gas, and vary greatly from person to person. Sufferers often experience swings from diarrhea to constipation. It is the most common disorder of the intestine, affecting 10 to 20 percent of adults, many of whom do not seek treatment. The cause of IBS, which strikes three times as many women as men, is unknown. Studies have suggested that anxious, compulsive, overconscientious, dependent, sensitive, guilt-ridden, unassertive, or depressed people may be more likely to develop IBS.

One problem facing doctors in trying to assess the role played by stress in IBS is that the disease itself causes stress. Patients may become caught in a cycle in which stress triggers IBS symptoms, which in turn exacerbate the stress.

Deep relaxation

The relaxation evoked through hypnosis will have a helpful effect on IBS symptoms. Hypnosis can teach IBS patients to use imagery to gain control over the muscles of the gut and bowel. The therapist talks patients into a calm and relaxed state, trying to get them to imagine their bowel muscles as very smooth and calm. Patients who successfully make use of the imagery report less pain, bloating, cramping, diarrhea, and constipation. More than three quarters of clients experience a marked improvement in their symptoms from direct hypnotic suggestion alone. Others can benefit from further psychotherapy.

Medical testimony

There are well documented medical studies of the benefits of hypnosis in IBS. In one study published in the *Lancet* in 1989, 33 people suffering from IBS were given four 40-minute sessions of hypnosis over seven weeks and taught self-hypnosis for twice-daily use at home. By the end of treatment, 20 of the 33 had improved, with 11 becoming almost symptom-free.

Stress can cause disturbances throughout the gastrointestinal tract that can be counteracted by hypnosis. Studies have also shown that hypnosis may be useful in maintaining remission in patients who have suffered from duodenal ulcers.

CASE STUDY: IBS

Stewart, aged 27, was a civil servant, and suffered from IBS. The fact that he could experience diarrhea at a moment's notice had led him to start mapping out his life according to where the nearest toilet was. He became so obsessed with fears that he might have an attack, that on occasion his anxiety would make his gut start to churn. He got to the point where he was becoming afraid to leave the house or take the bus to work. His lack of social life was starting to make him feel depressed, and he was becoming increasingly dependent on his elderly parents, with whom he still lived. His doctor, who first established that there was nothing physically wrong, recommended hypnosis.

Colon _____

Debate
Some scientists think that irritable bowel is the result of hormonal activity on the bowel wall, while others suggest that the central nervous system is involved.

Coping with Anxiety

TREATMENT

The therapist's first task when he put Stewart into hypnosis was to help him to feel relaxed, to stop him dwelling on his fears, and to break his obsession with toilets. The second was to give positive suggestions that his digestion would feel comfortable and relaxed so that his body would do its natural work. His subconscious was told that he would just go to the toilet when he needed to. As part of the treatment he agreed to confront his problems and begin to go out again. He was also given a self-hypnosis tape with suggestions for relaxation.

RESULTS

By the third session the suggestions were beginning to bite into Stewart's subconscious and have an effect. He was starting to go out with his friends again and happily making the journey to work. This saved him his job, which he had been in danger of losing due to his absences. By the fifth session his bowels had adopted a more or less normal pattern, and were having little effect on his life.

Stewart's sense of mental and physical well-being improved, as did his moods

His ability to cope with work returned

A lessening of symptoms allowed him to resume his social life

Restoration
Hypnosis broke the cycle of discomfort for Stewart and enabled him to get the routines of his life back to normal.

Headache and Migraine: Feedback Control

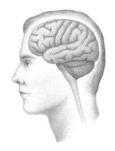

Tension
Some headaches are caused by a tightening of the muscles of the scalp.

Headaches are a common symptom experienced by 90 percent of the population at some time in their lives. Headaches can range in severity from a dull thudding in the temples to a frightening, intense pain. Often people know the cause—such as having too much to drink the night before. Other headaches, such as tension headaches, where the cause is not so obvious, are more frightening. Tension headaches—a sensation of tightness, pressure, or constriction—are caused by a tightening of muscles in the face, neck, and scalp as a result of stress or posture. The tension can cause muscles to contract and put pressures on arteries supplying the head, causing them to constrict.

Migraines

There is a considerable overlap between migraines and tension headaches, but if you experience two or more of the following symptoms together it is likely that you are suffering from migraines: visual disturbances such as blind spots or flashing lights, intense throbbing headaches often on one side of the head, nausea or vomiting, diarrhea, and increased sensitivity to light. Around one in ten people suffer from migraines.

Migraines are thought to result from spasm and dilation of the arteries and blood vessels supplying the brain. The cause of this remains unclear.

Reducing the pressure

Both migraines and headaches can
be helped by suggestions for relaxation
to make the patient feel less anxious.
Some therapists include suggestions that
the excessive blood in the head will
drain away.

   The treatment of a migraine by
biofeedback training to produce a
rise in the temperature of the hands and
arms is often applied without recourse
to formal hypnosis. In this method,
signals such as electronic bleeps,
flashes, or needles on a dial give the
sufferer clear "feedback" information
about the physical changes that they
are producing. The same approach
can be put to good use in hypnosis,
either by direct suggestion or,
alternatively, with the use of imagery
such as immersion of the hands in
warm water. Again, it is thought that
this technique works by reducing the
dilation of the cerebral vessels and
the pressure in them.

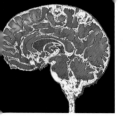

Causes
Migraines and headaches are thought to be caused by changes to the brain's blood supply.

CASE STUDY: HEADACHE
Sally, aged 40, was an administrator in social services, who experienced severe tension headaches. The headaches initially came once or twice a week, but then she started to wake up with them. Painkillers would ease them sufficiently to enable her to get to work, but by lunchtime she found that the pain would come back, and getting through the remainder of the day was a struggle. The headaches felt more like pressure around the orbital regions of her eyes and tension in her head and neck than an actual pain. She was stressed at work due to impossible deadlines that had been imposed on her by an unreasonable boss.

Causal factors
If there is underlying anxiety or depression— such as Sally's stress at work—causing tension headaches it needs to be addressed.

Self-help

Sally controlled her stress-related headaches with self-hypnosis techniques, which lessened the pain.

As her head cleared, her self-confidence improved

Self-hypnosis encouraged mental relaxation

Tension disappeared from Sally's neck and shoulders

Tension Prevention

TREATMENT

Sally had three sessions of hypnosis. As part of her induction the therapist used progressive muscular relaxation, in which he asked her to relax the muscles in her feet and then work all the way up her body. Once in hypnosis she used visual images of lying on a beach to achieve a dissociated daydreaming state that made her feel mentally relaxed. In hypnosis she was given suggestions that she would be more relaxed and calm at work in everything that she needed to do. She also practiced self-hypnosis at home whenever she felt tense.

RESULTS

By the third session Sally was starting to master the art of self-hypnosis to the extent that she could stop the tension building up in her head and neck and abort an attack. A follow-up session two months later showed that she had got the upper hand and was able to avoid getting into the tense state in the first place. The headaches had become a thing of the past for her. Knowing that she could master one of her problems had also increased Sally's confidence, and she was now thinking of changing jobs to escape her unreasonable boss.

Back Problems: Targeting Pain Relief

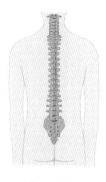

Delicate balance
*Any disturbance in the muscles
of the back results in problems
of the spine and nerves.*

Most of us will suffer from backaches at some time in our lives, and it is one of the most common reasons for people taking time off work. Backache is not an illness in itself, but only a symptom. Where it develops it usually means that something·has gone wrong somewhere, although it may not always be clear exactly what. It is estimated that anything up to one thousand million working days are lost per year in the US due to back pain.

Back problems may be due to a range of things from bad posture or incorrect lifting to damage to the spine. People most likely to suffer from back pain are those whose jobs involve much heavy lifting or carrying, or who spend long periods sitting in one position. The pain can be exaggerated by stress, anxiety, depression, and problems with marital relationships.

For some people, the tension and stress they experience in life seems to go straight to their backs. The result is that certain muscles contract, and since muscles generally work in pairs this can put the whole complex interacting system of muscles in the back out of kilter. When this leads to pressure being put on the nerves that come out of the spinal cord, the result is pain and tenderness over a wide area. Pain causes a vicious circle. Feeling pain makes the muscles tense up further and the situation escalates.

Progressive relaxation

Hypnosis can be used to target specific muscles and to give relaxing suggestions. Clients can be taken through a progressive exercise to aid relaxation of the back muscles. This will help to control the stresses that are bringing about the back problems. If the pain becomes chronic, methods such as hypnoanesthesia (see pages 148–149) can be used to control it. Many people find that hypnosis for back problems works best in combination with visiting a chiropractor, osteopath, or physical therapist.

Helping Yourself

How we stand and sit is important and may greatly affect our ability to cope with back pain. Taking care over your posture will minimize a lot of stresses on your spine.

Sit up straight
Sedentary jobs that involve long hours of bending over a desk will often result in back pain.

CASE STUDY: BACK PROBLEMS

Malcolm, aged 35, worked as a draftsman in a busy architect's office. His sedentary job involved sitting at a drawing board for long periods, and whenever there was any pressure such as urgent deadlines the problem seemed to go straight to the small of his back, where he would experience radiating pains. He experimented with different types of chairs, which for a time offered some relief, but in the long term the tension continued to build up.

Marvel
The back supports the body, bends and twists in all directions, and protects the nerves that run through it. With so many functions it is little wonder that it runs into trouble.

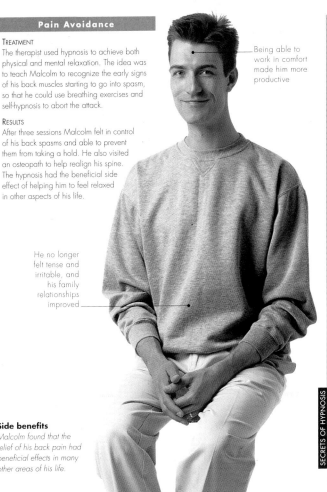

Pain Avoidance

TREATMENT

The therapist used hypnosis to achieve both physical and mental relaxation. The idea was to teach Malcolm to recognize the early signs of his back muscles starting to go into spasm, so that he could use breathing exercises and self-hypnosis to abort the attack.

RESULTS

After three sessions Malcolm felt in control of his back spasms and able to prevent them from taking a hold. He also visited an osteopath to help realign his spine. The hypnosis had the beneficial side effect of helping him to feel relaxed in other aspects of his life.

Being able to work in comfort made him more productive

He no longer felt tense and irritable, and his family relationships improved

Side benefits
Malcolm found that the relief of his back pain had beneficial effects in many other areas of his life.

Pain Relief: Altering Perception

Hypnosis is often more effective at pain relief than pain-relieving drugs such as codeine and morphine. The real advantage is that it is much safer, because hypnosis does not cause side effects, which impair your ability to make judgements or operate machinery, and is nonaddictive.

The Melzack and Wall gate-control theory of pain, first proposed in 1965, may help to explain why hypnosis helps to reduce pain. The theory—put forward after the recognition of the lack of a clear relationship between painful stimuli and the subjective experience of pain—proposes that input from the pain receptors passes through a gating mechanism in the spinal cord. The gate opens or closes depending on the distribution of activity in the ascending and descending nerve fibers.

The brain can respond to pain by releasing chemicals called endorphins, which reduce or inhibit pain sensations. Thus the gate may be influenced by

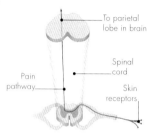

Pathway

The perception of pain originates from nerve endings that transmit electrical impulses to the brain.

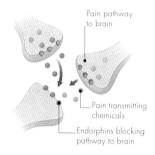

Prevention

This close-up of a nerve gate shows how endorphins can block further pain messages on their way to the brain.

both the peripheral response to a painful stimulus and higher brain activity such as cognition and emotion. The perceived intensity of the pain can be altered by the mental state, opening the way for psychological intervention.

Altering nerve messages

Hypnosis may work by encouraging the release of endorphins—the body's own painkillers—but the exact mechanism involved has not been established. When someone with chronic, long-term pain feels depressed, their relay station gates open more than usual, allowing more pain messages through. Because hypnosis can sometimes completely remove pain, or distract people from feeling it, it is important that a doctor assess the underlying medical or psychological condition prior to hypnosis. Getting rid of the pain when there is an important physical cause may prevent a condition from being properly treated.

PAIN-CONTROL TECHNIQUES

There are many different strategies therapists can use to reduce pain through hypnosis. Teaching people self-hypnosis transforms their attitude to pain. They no longer feel a victim, and take more control of their situation. Some of the most commonly used hypnotic techniques for pain control are outlined below.

Displacement

Suggestions that pain can move from one part of the body to another imply that alterations in other dimensions, such as the intensity of the pain, are possible. It is well known that pain in the extremities is less frightening than pain in the abdomen.

Dissociation

Asking the client to imagine that the pain goes elsewhere, leaving the physical body behind. Getting the client to engage in something interesting or enjoyable often helps.

Substitution

Substituting another sensation such as warmth for the pain, which helps the sufferer to reinterpret an unpleasant sensation.

Direct diminution

Suggesting that the pain will lessen and gradually go away, using metaphors such as "turning the volume down."

Glove anesthesia

Suggesting that the hand is numb, then transferring the feelings to any part of the body that you touch.

You can reduce pain by imagining feelings of happiness or comfort

Transference

Transfer feelings of numbness to painful areas.

Transform

Hypnosis deals with pain by altering our perception of it.

Neurophysiological metaphor

Asking the client to imagine a control panel in their brain on which they can turn down the pain-sending messages.

Creating a "visible form"

Giving the pain an imaginary shape or form to prevent it from seeming uncontrollable and unreachable.

Time distortion

Suggesting that when pain occurs, time will pass quickly, while during pain-free intervals time will pass slowly, giving a sense that comfort lasts longer than pain.

Age regression and progression

Going back to a time when the client had no pain, or going forward to a time in the future when they are pain free.

Reduce
Try imagining turning down the volume of your pain.

In a rush
Imagine time passing quickly at times of extreme pain.

You can imagine that a particular limb that is in pain is not part of your body

Hypnotic Anesthesia: Surgery without Pain

Skeptical
One of the hardest tasks can be convincing a surgeon to allow hypnosis in an operating theater.

Perhaps the most extreme example of the use of hypnosis for pain control is its use in surgical operations in place of anesthesia. For people who are allergic to anesthetics or extremely frail, hypnosis can have an important role to play in enabling them to undergo surgery without pain. The use of hypnosis in surgery dates back to the days before anesthetics. The first documented case, in 1829, is of a mastectomy performed by Jules Cloquet in France. Dr. James Esdaile, a Scottish surgeon working in India, used mesmerism in hundreds of operations. Later, hypnoanesthesia was used in the earliest open-heart surgeries, since general anesthesia was considered to carry too great a risk for such critically ill patients.

Modern times

Today only a handful of hypnotherapists offer this technique. Some therapists claim that only 10 percent of the population are actually capable of achieving the very deep levels of hypnosis that are required for surgery. This, however, is not the experience of John Butler who comments that "if people are suffering and hypnosis is the only way they can undergo surgery they will be extremely motivated to make the technique work."

Preparing for surgery

One of the keys to a successful analgesia is to allow a sufficient number of training sessions. During these, clients are taught some different techniques for pain removal, such as glove anesthesia (discussed on page 146). First, they are taught to control pain in small areas of their body, and once they are proficient in this they move on to control larger areas. Therapists satisfy themselves that clients are ready for surgery by testing the client with painful stimuli, such as a needle, to see whether they react. The advantages of using this kind of hypnosis in surgery include decreased anxiety and fear before the operation on the part of the patient, no toxic side effects, and beneficial effects on postoperative pain, discomfort, and nausea. The disadvantages are that the technique takes time to learn and you may not be able to arrange to have a therapist present during the surgery.

CASE STUDY: SURGERY

John, a 29-year-old bricklayer, needed an operation for an epigastric hernia that was bulging out from his abdominal wall. As a teenager he had been given a general anesthetic for a wisdom tooth extraction, and felt as though he had been "run over by a truck." For weeks afterward he felt nausea and lethargy, and was unable to sleep or eat properly. John was determined not to repeat the experience.

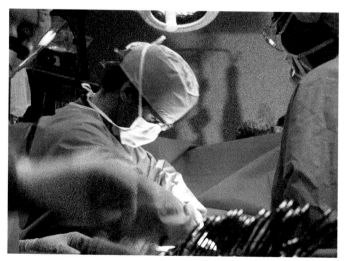

Alien environment
*Some patients find the clinical
environment off-putting and will need
plenty of reassurance.*

Power of Suggestion

TREATMENT

During hypnosis, John was given suggestions that he would experience no pain or discomfort or unnecessary sensations in the part of the body that the surgeons were working on. The therapist also used glove anesthesia to remove sensations of pain. At the end of five sessions the therapist was confident that John was receiving no sensations of pain from pins stuck into his abdomen and was ready for the operation.

RESULTS

After putting John into a relaxed state and using gloved anesthesia to remove any sensations in the abdominal region, the therapist continued to give him suggestions to reassure him.

The operation passed without a hitch and John reported no pain. At the end of the operation he was immediately able to move about freely and did not ask for pain relief. By the end of the week he was back playing sports.

Caution

John was advised not to talk during the operation since there is a danger that this can activate the conscious, analytical mind.

John's heart rate and blood pressure were monitored and remained steady

He indicated if he wanted to be taken deeper into the hypnosis by moving his hand

Childbirth: Managing Labor Pains

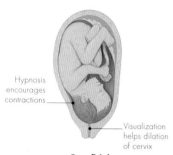

Hypnosis encourages contractions

Visualization helps dilation of cervix

Beneficial

Hypnosis helps to reduce high blood pressure, and may help to prevent premature delivery or to turn breech babies.

I f you are intending to use hypnosis in childbirth it is best to give yourself plenty of time to learn the technique before the birth. Try to start visiting a therapist in the fifth month of your pregnancy. Due to the unpredictable nature of labor, many women learn self-hypnosis, so that they do not need to rely on the presence of a therapist when the time comes.

Trance during labor

During the hypnotic sessions prior to the birth, some therapists will link contractions with deepening trance. The result is that by the time the woman goes into labor, it will be automatic for her to go into a deeper and deeper hypnotic trance whenever another contraction occurs.

During the birth itself, hypnosis can be used to relax the muscles in the first stage of labor when muscular tension exacerbates pain. Much of the pain experienced during childbirth is due to a woman's cultural expectation of birth being a painful event. The result is a vicious cycle of fear producing tension and pain, which results in more fear and stress, and more pain. The cycle can be broken by using hypnosis, which removes the tension and pain.

To help in the first stage of labor, a woman may find it helpful to visualize her cervix opening gently like a flower.

During the second stage of labor hypnosis can be useful in helping the womb muscles work at maximum efficiency when pushing the baby out. Some women find it helpful to visualize their contractions becoming strong and steady like powerful waves rolling in on the seashore. Hypnosis can also be used to produce distortions in time, helping mothers to feel that the labor has passed more quickly. After the birth, self-hypnosis could be used to stimulate breast milk and to help with the initial discomfort that most women experience when beginning breast-feeding.

It is important that women always inform their doctors that they are using self-hypnosis techniques. The danger is that, because you do not seem in much discomfort, you appear to be in a far earlier stage of labor than is actually the case. It is therefore important to have regular vaginal examinations to check how far the cervix has dilated.

CASE STUDY: CHILDBIRTH

Jill, a 26-year-old secretary, was pregnant with her first child. She had always been a worrier, and felt anxious that the pain of birth would detract from her enjoyment of the process. She was concerned that her threshold for pain was low, but did not like the idea of the adverse effect that pain relief might have on her baby. She thought hypnosis sounded much more effective than deep breathing, and was something that she could learn in order to help herself. Jill was also keen to breast-feed her baby, but had heard reports from friends that the experience could be remarkably uncomfortable in the first few days during which the baby is perfecting its technique. She was also concerned that she would find the sleep deprivation particularly hard, and she thought that learning hypnosis would help her through the tricky first few weeks of motherhood.

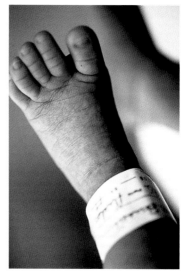

Joy
The feelings of relaxation induced by hypnosis can help mothers enjoy their first few hours of parenthood.

In Control

TREATMENT

Jill first saw a hypnotherapist in the sixth month of her pregnancy. She was helped to relax and given posthypnotic suggestions to replace any fears with positive, confident thoughts, and to encourage her to relax with each contraction, to flow with them and not to resist them.

She was taught to use glove anesthesia as a method of pain control. The therapist, who was not going to be present at the birth, prepared self-hypnosis tapes to use in both the first and second stages of her labor.

RESULTS

Through the first stage of labor, the tape gave suggestions for strength and stamina. In the second stage another tape gave her suggestions that her body knew what it was doing and that she should just go with it. Her first stage only lasted six hours from start to finish, which is quick for a first labor, and she was delighted that she managed to avoid an epidural and get by with just having the occasional whiff of trylene.

Babies born using hypnosis are thought to be more alert than other newborns

Calming
Self-hypnosis can help you to cope with the stress and sleep deprivation of the early days of parenthood.

Dentistry: Dealing with Phobias

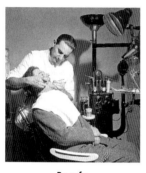

Be safe

Before allowing your dentist to perform hypnosis, check that they are a member of a professional body that recognizes their techniques.

Hypnosis can be used in dentistry both for its tranquilizing effects in calming people down before the procedure and in place of anesthesia. It can be performed by the dentist while you are in the chair, or by a hypnotherapist prior to your visit.

Altering pain perception

The aim of hypnosis in dentistry is to teach people to cope with the situation to the best of their ability. The pain involves not only the actual component of pain you experience, but the anticipated pain compounded by your anxiety and fear. The starting point for therapy is the reduction of fear and tension, producing relaxation and breaking the fear–tension–pain–fear cycle. Posthypnotic suggestions can be used to make people feel relaxed as soon as they sit in the dental chair. Other helpful techniques include suggestions that every ten minutes in the dentist's chair will feel like one minute.

None of us likes going to the dentist, but for some people it is one of the most stressful events they can experience and they develop a severe phobia. The result is that they avoid going to the dentist for regular dental checkups, and as a consequence the condition of their teeth deteriorates.

Hypnotic suggestions can also be used to reduce bleeding. Dentists who practice hypnosis can find it valuable to include suggestions for patients to floss their teeth regularly and to encourage them to come back for the next appointment within the set time period.

Medical testimony

In one study, dentists from Sweden divided 70 patients about to undergo wisdom tooth extractions into two groups. One group was sent home and told to report on the day of the operation, while the others were given audio tapes with hypnotic suggestions for relaxation and pain relief. After surgery the patients were asked about their reactions to the surgery and their recoveries. The researchers found that the group who had listened to the tape experienced less anxiety before the operation, less bleeding during surgery, and needed less pain relief and had lower rates of infection afterward.

CASE STUDY: DENTISTRY

Tom, a 24-year-old pharmacist, had a dental phobia stemming from a bad childhood experience with a dentist. The dentist had been rough and started working before the anesthetic had a chance to take hold. Over the years, Tom's fear of dentists built up until it became exaggerated out of all proportion. He had not been to the dentist in more than five years and needed two extractions and three fillings. But the idea of even telephoning the dentist to make an appointment was enough to produce a panic attack.

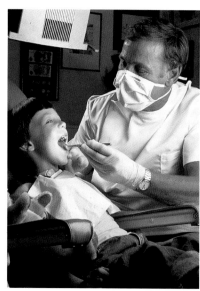

Reassuring
Helping children to feel comfortable with visiting the dentist can prevent phobias in later life.

TREATMENT
The goal of the hypnotherapist was to produce a more realistic, positive attitude to dentistry. Tom was given suggestions that he would feel calm and relaxed at the dentist's, and that he would not suffer discomfort and would know that he was in good hands.

RESULTS
After the second session of hypnosis, Tom felt ready to make his dental appointment. After a further two sessions designed to give him confidence he went for his appointment. He found that he had overcome the negative thoughts and could tolerate the work being done. At the end of the treatment, although he did not positively enjoy the experience, going to the dentist no longer frightened him.

Dissociation
Hypnosis removed Tom's association of the dentist with an unpleasant experience in his childhood.

Tom's fears were calmed by reprogramming his attitudes

He kept his teeth in good condition after the treatment

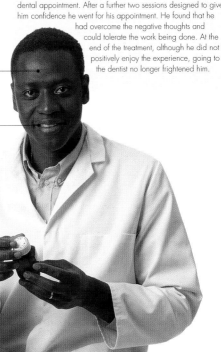

Cancer: Support During Treatment

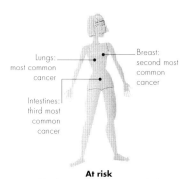

Lungs: most common cancer

Breast: second most common cancer

Intestines: third most common cancer

At risk

This diagram shows the sites at which cancerous tumors are most likely to occur.

Cancer occurs when cells in the body start to multiply out of control and escape the body's complex system of checks. Cancer will affect one in three of the population at some time in their lives, and as the population ages the incidence is rising.

Hypnosis can be used in a number of ways to help people through the different stages of cancer. It helps to reduce the stress, lessens the side effects of treatment, and enhances feelings of well-being. It can help people to feel more in control, because it is something they can do for themselves. It is important to appreciate that hypnosis does not take the place of conventional therapies for cancer, but adds to them.

Enhancing coping skills

People with cancer may face intense fears, anxieties, and frustrations. They are on a constant rollercoaster of hope and despair, courage and fear. Hypnosis can be helpful in alleviating the initial anxiety that accompanies diagnosis. It can be used to reduce anxiety by identifying stressful situations in the patient's life, desensitizing the patient to them, and enhancing their coping skills. Hypnosis can be used to help patients to feel more confident about treatments such as radiation and chemotherapy. Suggestions can be used to help side effects such as nausea and vomiting. Hypnotic suggestions for reframing can help people to come to terms with their altered body images. Some practitioners also claim that relaxation techniques, particularly the use of imagery, can prolong life by boosting the immune system. There is currently insufficient evidence to establish the validity of this claim.

Medical testimony

Debilitating pain is reported by 60 to 90 percent of patients with advanced cancer. Most receive painkillers such as morphine, but some experts now believe they could benefit further by adding hypnosis to their treatment. In 1992, researchers at the Fred Hutchinson Cancer Research Center in Seattle found that hypnosis, used together with pain medication, was more effective than other psychological interventions or painkilling drugs in reducing oral discomfort in people who had undergone bone marrow transplants for leukemia.

CASE STUDY: CANCER

Susan, 34, was diagnosed with the late stages of ovarian cancer, which had spread to her liver. She was told that her condition was terminal and that she had only a few months to live. She decided that she wanted help from hypnosis to make sense of why it had happened to her and to get over her feelings of shock and depression. She also wanted help with the pain which was becoming uncomfortable due to a buildup of fluid in her abdomen.

Complementary therapies

When conventional medicine fails to help terminal patients, hypnosis can add invaluable support in helping them come to terms with their situation.

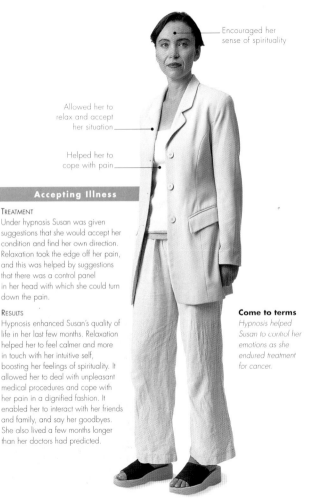

Encouraged her
sense of spirituality

Allowed her to
relax and accept
her situation

Helped her to
cope with pain

Accepting Illness

TREATMENT

Under hypnosis Susan was given
suggestions that she would accept her
condition and find her own direction.
Relaxation took the edge off her pain,
and this was helped by suggestions
that there was a control panel
in her head with which she could turn
down the pain.

RESULTS

Hypnosis enhanced Susan's quality of
life in her last few months. Relaxation
helped her to feel calmer and more
in touch with her intuitive self,
boosting her feelings of spirituality. It
allowed her to deal with unpleasant
medical procedures and cope with
her pain in a dignified fashion. It
enabled her to interact with her friends
and family, and say her goodbyes.
She also lived a few months longer
than her doctors had predicted.

Come to terms

*Hypnosis helped
Susan to control her
emotions as she
endured treatment
for cancer.*

The Immune System: Going into Battle

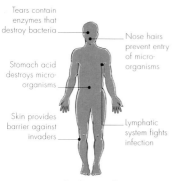

Tears contain enzymes that destroy bacteria

Nose hairs prevent entry of micro-organisms

Stomach acid destroys micro-organisms

Skin provides barrier against invaders

Lymphatic system fights infection

Battleground

When the body's defenses are breached, the immune system engulfs or neutralizes invaders with antibodies.

The actions of the immune system are very complex. When antigens (foreign proteins) invade the body, cells known as B-lymphocytes (B-cells) multiply, forming plasma cells which produce antibodies to destroy the invaders. After B-cells have killed the bacteria, some remain in the body as memory cells that can spring into action if the antigen is ever found again.

The production of B-cells is controlled by a second group of cells known as T-lymphocytes (T-cells), which switch B-cells on and off. One type of T-cell plays a role in destroying the body's own cells if they are infected by a virus or turn cancerous. These "killer" cells can recognize and destroy foreign material even if they have not encountered it before. Some cancer cells are recognized as foreign by killer cells and destroyed, so the ability to buffer the decline of or raise the count of killer cells has important implications. There is evidence that certain hormones released in response to stress, such as epinephrine, interfere with the ability of T-cells and B-cells to divide and multiply. Relaxation brought about by hypnotherapy may help to counter this.

Medical testimony

In the 1980s, experiments on blood samples taken from students at Ohio State University showed that during stressful events such as exams, activity in the killer cells was reduced. They went on to show a positive correlation between the amount of self-hypnosis practiced by students during exam time and their killer cell counts.

The British professor Leslie Walker has demonstrated the value of psychological interventions with oncology patients. In a recent study, 80 women with advanced breast cancer were divided into two groups. The first group received support from the team, while the second received support plus training in progressive muscular relaxation and the use of guided imagery. The additional intervention enhanced mood and quality of life, helped coping strategies, and had an effect on the immune system—patients receiving the additional interventions had higher numbers of T-cells. However, there is currently no direct evidence that the effects of psychological interventions on immune defense prolong survival.

Imagery
A popular visualization image used by cancer patients is a shoal of fish nibbling away at the tumor.

VISUALIZATION TREATMENT
Some people with cancer find it helpful to create a picture in their mind of their condition and the forces they are marshalling against it. An image may send a message from the cerebral cortex via the lower brain to the hormonal system and the autonomic nervous system, which may in turn influence the immune system. This area is part of the new discipline of psychoneuroimmunology, which is the scientific study of the interrelations between the mind and the nervous, endocrine (hormonal), and immune systems.

Phagocytes
When the goal is to boost the immune system, some people find that guided imagery directed toward mobilizing the immune system is helpful. One aspect of the immune system that can be visual and therefore easier to focus on is the action of cells called phagocytes. These white blood cells are attracted to infection sites, where they engulf and digest microorganisms. The phagocyte first recognizes the invading cells as foreign. Next they engulf the invading cells in a pouch. Finally, enzymes in fluid-filled particles move toward the tumor and are released into the pouch where they start to digest foreign material.

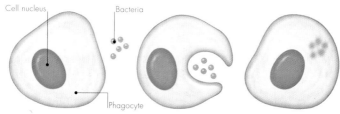

Cell nucleus

Bacteria

Phagocyte

The battle

Another useful image is of your body defending itself stoically from attack. The patient imagines an army of immune cells, which look like strong, vigorous soldiers, overcoming and destroying the weaker, gray-colored abnormal cells.

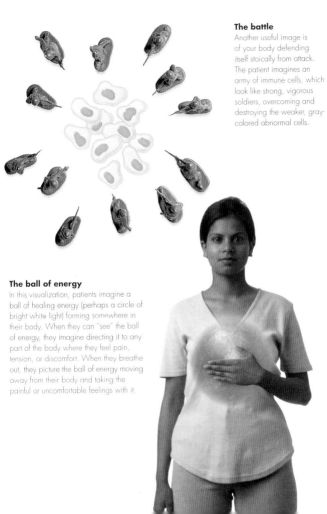

The ball of energy

In this visualization, patients imagine a ball of healing energy (perhaps a circle of bright white light) forming somewhere in their body. When they can "see" the ball of energy, they imagine directing it to any part of the body where they feel pain, tension, or discomfort. When they breathe out, they picture the ball of energy moving away from their body and taking the painful or uncomfortable feelings with it.

Hypnosis in Surgery: Additional Applications

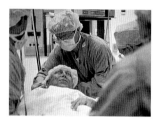

Assistance

Hypnosis is used to reduce anxiety before surgery and help people endure days of discomfort afterward.

In the field of surgery, hypnosis is not only used in place of anesthesia, but can increase the speed of recovery, boost the immune system, and help control postoperative nausea. There is evidence that it can be used to reduce the amount of blood lost during surgery.

The prospect of an operation is an event that hangs over people like a dark cloud. Hypnosis can be used to reduce their anxiety and help give them a positive outlook and even an enthusiasm for the experience. Hypnotic suggestions can be given to make the patient feel calm and comfortable before, during, and after the operation.

Other helpful approaches include suggesting that if the patient hears any negative comments during the operation, they will ignore them. Since awareness under anesthesia is considered possible, off-hand comments made by operating staff could adversely affect recovery.

Quick recovery

After surgery hypnosis can help recovery from the anesthetic, and reduce or eliminate postoperative pain and the need for painkillers. It can also be used to control nausea, vomiting, and bowel distress. Healing suggestions can be used to help boost the immune system. In the recovery period, hypnosis can create a positive outlook and avoid any focus on negative emotions, which could depress the immune system. In a study comparing 15 patients undergoing open heart surgery, 8 of the group listened to relaxation tapes before their operations and 7 did not. The group using the tapes had fewer negative psychological reactions and a shorter recovery period from analgesia, and needed fewer blood transfusions.

Scientific testimony

A Swedish study looking at surgery for facial reconstruction showed that blood loss was reduced in the patients who received hypnosis prior to the operation, compared with the control group. Since blood vessels are under autonomic control it is reasonable to assume that the subconscious mind could be taught to make them contract, thereby reducing blood flow.

Pain Control

In the 1960s and 1970s Dr. Jack Gibson, an Irish surgeon, performed over 4,000 surgical operations, using hypnosis as the anesthetic.

PERFORMANCE
ENHANCEMENT

Confidence and motivation have a key role to play in getting the best out of all performances. Whether you are an athlete running a race, an actor playing a role, a composer writing a symphony, or a student studying for an exam, hypnosis can be used to help you prioritize and achieve your goals. Above all it makes people confident by preventing destructive feelings of self-doubt, allowing them to keep their anxiety at exactly the right level to achieve the best results. Anxiety is essentially a learned and anticipatory response, in contrast to fear which is a more innate emotion. For people to exert themselves fully in pursuing various goals, whether athletic, academic, or creative, it is necessary for them to experience some degree of arousal. However, each of us has an optimal level of arousal for a given situation, and if it rises too high it inhibits rather than aids performance.

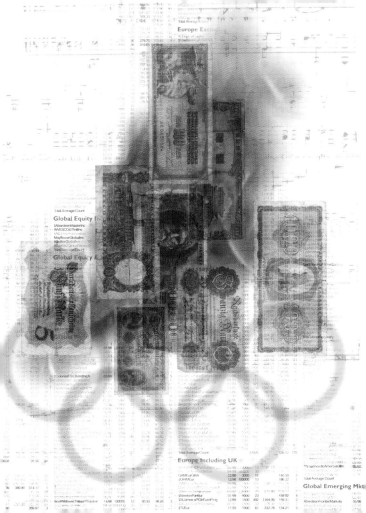

Why Some People Lack Confidence

Take heart
If you believe in yourself you will have an easier job persuading others of your ability.

A major goal of hypnosis is to improve your self-esteem and confidence. If you truly believe in your own abilities, you will find it much easier to persuade other people of them. Feeling good about yourself will have a valuable additional effect in many areas of your life, from improving your relationships with colleagues, to helping to persuade clients to buy products, and even helping you to have a successful love life. It will undoubtedly help with assertiveness—if you believe in yourself you will feel far more capable of standing up for your rights even in confrontational situations.

Self-esteem

A lack of self-esteem is often something that is deeply rooted in a person's past. It can be a style of thinking inherited from judgmental parents, who continually put their child down to persuade her to work harder. This can lead to the acquirement of a critical inner voice which produces internal fear and feelings of self-doubt.

Fear of failure is an immobilizing condition that is the product of past negative programming. People fear that they will not be able to accomplish certain tasks because they are not worthy of accomplishing them. Furthermore, they can tell themselves that if they manage to succeed at one level, they will only then have to

succeed at a higher level next time.
Self-esteem can also be affected by the
way people perceive themselves
physically. If they view their appearance
in a negative light, this is likely to reflect
in their body language, and will make
them appear far less confident.

Social phobia

An extreme lack of confidence which
causes someone to go out of their way
to avoid social gatherings is called
social phobia. The patient may worry
about being the center of attention and
may feel that everyone is scrutinizing
their behavior. Around 2 percent of men
and 3 percent of women suffer from
severe social phobia, and a further 7
percent of the population show a
tendency toward it. Nobody really
knows why people develop social
phobia—some psychologists believe
that they get stuck in the normal stage
of shyness and fear of strangers, which
all children experience.

IMPROVING SELF-ESTEEM

One way to improve your self-esteem is through hypnotic suggestions where you re-program your subconscious mind to remove any past negative programming. Hypnosis can be used to banish your inner critic on so that you see yourself in the most positive light possible. Rather than putting up road blocks and saying you cannot do something, hypnosis can implant positive thoughts such as "I can do it," "I have the energy," or "I am just right for the job." Through positive suggestions given during hypnosis you can start to see yourself as confident, and become certain of your own abilities and talents.

Confidence

*Hypnosis can help you to project yourself in a
positive light. You can be given hypnotic suggestions
that you enjoy socializing and feel calm, confident,
and at ease in your interactions with other people.*

Self-belief
Hypnosis can be used to increase your confidence and self-acceptance by asking you to imagine yourself standing tall and being who you really are.

Eraser
Under hypnosis the therapist may ask you to visualize a blackboard with all the uncomfortable labels that have been given to you in the past written on it.

In your imagination you rub out the negative words from your mind so that they have no meaning for you.

Performing at Sports: Sharpening Your Focus

Gets rid of shaky hands

Removes butterflies in the stomach

Staying focused

Hypnotic suggestions can be used to prevent physical symptoms from getting in the way of good performance.

Creating focus

Before a sports event, the mere thought of failing can be enough to trigger feelings of fear. This will cause the athlete to lose focus, and can lead to physical symptoms such as feeling weak at the knees, butterflies in the stomach, and blurred vision. Hypnosis can be used to focus the attention.

After an extended bout of bad luck, the athlete's consequent negative outlook can be changed through hypnosis. Confidence-building through ego-strengthening messages can be used to program athletes with winning attitudes. Trigger words can be implanted as posthypnotic suggestions, and when the athlete repeats them in competition they will provide a surge of energy and confidence.

Visual imagery

Visual imagery used to enhance an athletic performance can be either internal, when athletes feel as though

To compete in any national or international competition, athletes need to be exceptional at their game or event. The consequence is that the physical skills of top athletes are virtually identical and the principal difference between winners and losers is mental focus. Hypnosis can be used to give a mental edge.

they are inside their own bodies, or external, when they "watch" themselves from the outside. Kay Porter and Judy Foster, authors of the book *The Mental Athlete*, have suggested that visualizing specific movements from the inside creates neural patterns of them in the brain, improving neuromuscular co-ordination. Since it is the brain that tells the muscles when and how to move, the stronger the patterns, the more perfect the movement is likely to be.

In addition, if you run mental "films" of your own success, the subconscious mind becomes convinced that a desired feat is possible. A study in the US in the 1960s gave basketball players sessions with a hypnotist, in which they received suggestions for playing a better game and visualizing themselves winning. When their shooting scores were compared with the scores of a comparable group of players who had not been exposed to hypnosis, they were found to be appreciably better.

On the ball
Golfers can practice visualizing hitting the ball even when they are not on the course.

CASE STUDY: SPORT
Many golfers, even professionals, find that they can be great on the practice range, but terrible on the golf course. Hypnotism can bring enormous benefits to the game of golf, which is perhaps more a question of mental skill than any other sport. It is a game in which people need to stay calm and maintain high levels of concentration for long periods of time. They also need high levels of self-confidence to stay calm in the face of the opposition.

Nerves
Golf is a game where so much hangs on a particular putt that it is little wonder that professional players become anxious.

Teeing Off

TREATMENT

Hypnosis can be used to help golfers control their emotions and prevent any other thoughts from getting in the way. It can be used to prevent them from being intimidated by opponents. Relaxation techniques can block out noises that could disturb their concentration. Suggestions can be given that the body is capable of performing the necessary skills. Finally, visualizations can be performed to rehearse swinging the clubs mentally.

RESULTS

Hypnosis can bring about an improvement in swing and one's accuracy of hitting the ball. It produces the right degree of tension in the muscles, and helps players judge how hard they will have to hit the ball against the wind. It helps players to keep calm when under pressure to sink a ball. Players become altogether more successful because of a more positive mental outlook. Hypnosis breaks their mind-set of fear and the stress/tension cycle.

Winner

When the professional golfer Bernhard Langer hit a bad patch he enlisted the services of a hypnotist. He soon experienced a marked improvement in his game.

Performing at Work: Visualizing Success

Power of suggestion
Hypnosis will program your subconscious mind for success.

In business, people can be taught self-hypnosis to program their subconscious mind for greater success. They can program themselves to appear confident with clients. Hypnosis can also be used to help them handle rejection in a more constructive fashion, and to avoid feelings of failure. For motivation, business people can use visualization to imagine the direct benefits they will receive from success. They can picture things they would like in their future, such as a new home, a vacation, or a car.

Many people from history with a tremendous capacity for work and leadership, such as Caesar, Napoleon, and Leonardo da Vinci, had personal qualities in common, including an unfailing confidence in themselves, unusual powers of mental concentration, retentive memories, and the ability to influence others. Many of these things can be enhanced through hypnosis.

Positive visualization

Implanting positive suggestions under hypnosis can help people acquire a more positive attitude to a job they dislike. It can also help bosses manage staff more effectively, and help managers build on their empathic skills so that they have a greater ability to know what the team is feeling. Hypnotic suggestions can also be used to help people stay calm and focused during interviews. Visualizing the scene in advance enables them to present exactly the image they want to the interview panel, and to avoid nervous gestures such as throat-clearing and blushing. Visualization can also make people feel calm and collected when giving lectures or speaking in public in meetings or at conferences. They can imagine themselves addressing a large audience and feeling confident and at ease, and can be given suggestions that they will enjoy the experience.

Hypnosis can help you to make effective decisions in every area of working life, from filing to prioritizing your workload. It can help you to deal with distractions, and to be assertive in saying no to people who monopolize your time. It can help to motivate you to meet your deadlines. In addition, hypnosis can help when your creativity feels as though it has dried up (see pages 184–185).

Negative spiral
Nigel's increasing lack of confidence was affecting his performance at work.

CASE STUDY: WORK

Nigel, 25, was a salesman selling life insurance, personal pensions, and investment packages. The industry was going through a bad patch, and Nigel had suffered a run of bad luck. This had knocked his confidence and made him doubt his ability to do the job. He started to find it difficult to be assertive and entered a negative spiral in which his poor achievements led to low expectations, which led to further underperformance. Clients were beginning to pick up on his hesitation and negativity and his sales were going down. He was beginning to lose confidence and his belief in the products he was selling. He got to the point at which he felt in danger of losing his job, and needed to find a solution.

Under pressure
Work conflicts place people under considerable stress that can spill over into other areas of their lives.

Mental boost

Nigel needed to recover his confidence, and hypnosis provided the boost he was looking for by changing his attitude.

He made better eye contact with his clients

His body language became more relaxed

He came across as friendly and approachable and his explanations became clearer

Break the Cycle

TREATMENT

Under hypnosis Nigel was given direct re-programming to make him believe that he was capable of doing well, and to boost his feelings of self-confidence. He was given direct suggestions that he felt confident when in front of people, and could deal intelligently with their questions. He was made to feel that he would perform better with each day that went by. Altogether he had five sessions of hypnosis and took a tape home to practice.

RESULTS

From the first session Nigel began to feel more confident about his work and better able to make cold calls. His belief in his products started to come across to his clients, and he answered their questions eloquently. He achieved real results, with his sales going up, and clients started to recommend him to their friends. He kept his job and felt so confident that he found the courage to ask his boss for a transfer to the area of the country where he really wanted to work.

Enhancing Your Latent Creativity

E = mc²

Albert Einstein's best ideas came while shaving. The repetitive action of shaving is rather hypnotic, and can allow new thoughts to rise to the surface.

Creativity allows our imagination to produce fresh insights and revolutionary ideas. It is surprising how many of the world's best ideas have come when their creators have been in a trancelike state. Beethoven and Darwin had many of their ideas while riding in carriages, Archimedes while sitting in a bath tub, and Einstein while shaving. Mozart described how ideas came to him from an external source when he was in a dreamlike state. Most of us are familiar with critical insights occurring at unexpected times and places. Often we become totally immersed in a problem and approach it from all possible angles without finding a solution, but during a period of relaxation afterward, the very idea we have been seeking emerges.

Generally, the creative process is poorly understood. A high score on an intelligence test does not automatically indicate a high degree of creativity. In fact, top scorers on creativity tests average 23 IQ points lower than top scorers on intelligence tests. This may explain why the subconscious mind (the right hemisphere of the brain) is thought to be the source of creative expression, while the conscious, logical mind (the left hemisphere) which handles day-to-day business such as talking, writing, and reasoning, has little role to play.

Highly creative people, such as writers, artists, and musicians, can suffer from blocks when their creative imagination suddenly dries up. The harder they seek for inspiration, the more difficult it becomes to find it. Creative abilities can also be adversely affected by fear and self-criticism. Many artists will be all too familiar with the internal voice saying "What you are doing is just not good enough."

Awakening inspiration

Hypnosis can relax creative people and allow a way of contacting the right side of the brain to achieve the best mental state for inspiration. Suggestions may include: "You feel all of your creative energy rising to the surface." Ego-boosting may also help, with suggestions that they are an excellent, highly talented writer. Writers can also be helped by specific suggestions that whenever they sit at their desk to write, ideas will flow.

CASE STUDIES: CREATIVITY

Throughout history, writers, artists, and musicians have embraced hypnosis as a way to boost their creativity, overcome artistic blocks, and promote feelings of confidence in their abilities.

Unblock

Musicians, artists, and writers can use self-hypnosis to gain inner passion for work they have grown weary of.

Release

The composer Sergei Rachmaninov (1873–1943) suffered a three-year unproductive period after the failure of his First Symphony in 1897. Following hypnosis treatment, he produced the successful Second Piano Concerto in 1901, and this inspired a period of creativity that lasted until 1917.

Case history

After ten unsuccessful years in acting, hypnosis tapes gave Sylvester Stallone the courage to submit a script about an up-and-coming boxer to Hollywood. But even after his big break Stallone feared that he did not have the talent to pull off a major picture. Every day while shooting "Rocky" he listened to motivational tapes to boost his confidence.

Enhancing Your Learning Power

Study time

Hypnosis can help eliminate distractions and make you more flexible in your thinking.

A growing area of interest is the use of hypnosis to help concentration, attention, and stamina in educational and academic settings. Techniques can be used to make students feel more relaxed so that they will be able to get through their work with less stress than they would otherwise have experienced. It can also help to ease the problem created by low self-esteem, lack of motivation, and poor study skills.

Clear thinking

Hypnosis can help people to be more effective and flexible in their thinking and to find solutions to difficulties. It can eliminate external distractions during study periods, and, for people who find it hard to sit still in lectures, self-hypnosis can help them feel that the time is passing more quickly.

A more controversial subject in this area is whether hypnosis has any effect on boosting memory. Some researchers have claimed that it is not directly effective in improving memory, but others disagree. The problem with laboratory studies of this is that everyone is given a standard script that is not tailored to individual needs.

Exams

Taking exams is a very anxious time, particularly when students realize that much of their future life depends on the results. Hypnosis can be valuable to help manage exam anxiety, particularly for people who know their material well but do badly in exams because of nerves. Anticipatory anxiety before exams can be reduced with desensitization techniques. In hypnosis before exams, students can be given suggestions that they will sleep easily, that they will feel calm before the exam, and that their memory is excellent.

Students can be taught anxiety-management routines for use at the start of exams. One such technique is self-hypnosis in which you place a hand momentarily over your eyes and think of a key word that has been given to you during a hypnosis session to promote feelings of instant relaxation. Another technique is the clenched fist. Here the student enters an hypnotic trance, recalls a situation when they felt confident and relaxed, then makes a fist with their right hand. The idea is that whenever they close their hand into a fist they will experience those uplifting feelings once again.

HYPNOSIS
FOR CHILDREN

Children are often the best hypnotic subjects. Hypnosis is easier for them because they are accustomed to switching between reality and fantasy, and have more fertile imaginations. One of the earliest examples of hypnosis in life is the interaction between mother and child, since the child is very open to suggestions. If the child injures itself and the mother says "I'll kiss it better," the child will take the suggestion instantly and forget their pain. Parents also use a form of hypnosis with infants by gently rocking them to sleep. Unlike adults, who usually remember everything about an hypnosis session, children often remember little. The body relaxation normally associated with adult sessions is also less evident in children, who may remain surprisingly active throughout.

Habit Disorders: Treating Tension and Anxiety

Treatment

In children, hypnosis can help to tackle undesirable habits ranging from nailbiting to sleepwalking and substance abuse.

Dispelling the tension

Many habit disorders develop in order to discharge underlying tension. Hypnotherapeutic treatments aim to extinguish the habit and teach other more effective ways of discharging tension and anxiety. Fantasy methods to decrease anxiety and tension include imagining the boiler of an old engine letting off steam.

Often, even when the origin of an undesirable habit is no longer present, the behavior may continue to exist once anxiety begins to assert itself again, or distractions are lessened. Children often revert to hairpulling or nailbiting while watching television or reading. Imagery can help for some, such as suggesting a force field preventing the child from pulling his or her hair. Hypnosis for bedwetting works well when other traditional methods, such as the pad and buzzer, have proved unsuccessful. Suggestion is given that when they feel the need to go to the toilet they will

Hypnosis can be used to treat various habit disorders in children, such as bedwetting, facial tics, and sleepwalking. If the habit is fed by dysfunctional relationships or other emotional problems, additional psychological work may be necessary. Always consult your doctor before taking a child to a hypnotherapist.

wake up. It is important that the child sees the advantages in being dry and the disadvantages in continuing to be wet. In 1975, a study of 40 children aged between the ages of 4 and 16 using self-hypnosis, found that after six months 31 of the children had stopped bedwetting, 6 had improved and 3 had not.

Hypnosis has also been used to help children with undesirable habits, certain addictions, and various behavioral problems including antisocial and disruptive behavior, and dangerous activities such as glue-sniffing. In a 1982 study, six adolescents who had a long history of substance abuse and had failed to respond to other treatments were given hypnosis, while six matched control subjects were not. At the end of 15 weeks, all of the teenagers in the first group had stopped abusing solvents, while only two of the control group had successfully stopped.

CASE STUDY: BEDWETTING
Jack, a bright eight-year-old, was mature for his age, yet still experienced a persistent problem of bedwetting. Every few mornings he would wake to find his bed completely soaked. This caused him considerable embarrassment in front of his two older brothers, who would tease him about being a "baby." In the morning rush his mother also sometimes failed to hide her irritation about the amount of laundry this produced. Things came to a head when Jack had to make up an excuse for not going to his best friend's pajama party. He became depressed and withdrawn. His mother decided that the problem really needed to be dealt with and enlisted the help of a hypnotherapist.

Good subjects
Studies have shown that responsiveness to hypnosis peaks in middle childhood and is followed by a gradual decline toward adulthood.

A Problem Solved

TREATMENT

Jack was mature enough to internalize imaginative involvement, and could focus his attention on fantasies and images. The hypnotist used the induction technique of getting him to imagine that he was visiting the fun fair and going on different rides such as the big dipper. Once he was under, the therapist used the direct suggestion that if Jack felt sensations of fullness in his bladder at any time during the night he would immediately wake up.

RESULTS

At the second session, which was held two weeks later, Jack reported that he had managed to go for six nights before having a problem and that he was regularly waking during the night. At the third session he reported that he had remained dry for over two weeks. At his six-month follow-up he was happy to report that he no longer had the problem and was feeling confident enough to go to scout camp in the summer.

His confidence increased

He woke up whenever his bladder felt full

Recovery
After hypnotism, Jack gradually left the problem of bedwetting behind him, and with it, the teasing from his brothers.

Education: Helping the Learning Process

Positive
It is important for teachers to implant constant suggestions for success.

Hypnosis can be used to enhance learning at any stage of a child's education. Some believe that it helps by enabling both halves of the brain to function in an integrated way. If children develop a bad reaction to one subject area, hypnosis can be used to overcome it by programming them into positive ways of thinking. For children with learning difficulties, which also tend to lead to poor self-image, anxiety-reduction and ego-strengthening techniques can prove helpful.

Looking at the background

Family problems can be very unsettling, and therapy may also need to address these factors. For anxiety, lack of confidence, fear of failure, or other emotional problems, hypnosis can be very useful provided that the child is mature enough to understand the therapist's interventions. The therapist needs to communicate in a manner appropriate to the level of the child's development.

Children who have problems dealing with authority figures may be paralyzed with fear at the thought of speaking to the teacher and appear dumb in class. This needs to be tackled in childhood or they will grow into adults who fear or resent authority figures. To get them over such problems, role playing during hypnosis may help.

Many children find that when they do their homework their attention wanders. Hypnosis can help focus them. Many teenagers do poorly in exams because of anxiety; therapists can suggest that they are relaxed and confident, and will perform well on the test.

Practical examples

In Sweden, teachers routinely take children through a hypnotic drill before lessons start in which they give them suggestions about enjoying their work. One study in a New York school used hypnotism with 48 children who were having trouble in school because of poor attention spans. Every morning their teacher played a 15-minute audio tape that hypnotized them and gave them suggestions that they would feel relaxed and learn as well as the other children. At the end of the year, 45 of these children showed improvements in their schoolwork and attention spans and were less distracted.

$$(x+h)^2 = k$$

$$2x^2 + 12x - 3 = 0$$

$$x^2 + 6x - 1.5 =$$

$$(x+3)^2 = 10.5$$

$$x + 3 = \pm 3.24$$

$$x = 0.24$$

$$\text{or } x = -6.24$$

$$x + 3y = 11$$

$$5x - 2y = 4$$

$$5x + 15y = 55$$

$$17y = 51$$

$$y = 3$$

$$x + 3 \times 3 =$$

$$x = 2$$

Bright spark
Getting a young child to gaze at a flashlight is one way of inducing trance.

SPECIAL METHODS
Language, techniques, and images must be selected to match the developmental level of the child. To use most hypnotic techniques, a child must be old enough to listen to a story. The task of catching his attention and using his absorption in a fantasy to modify his behavior is then possible. Young children respond very well to the storytelling technique rather than more formal hypnotic methods. Therapeutic suggestions for well-being, analgesia, or improvement of the presenting problem can be embedded into the story.

Fear cure
Children can be helped to overcome phobias, such as arachnophobia, by drawing the feared object.

Child-friendly Methods

HYPNOTIC HEROES
The hypnotic hero technique involves using the
child's favorite heroes from television,
cartoons, and books to help the child with
their problem. The therapist may deliver
suggestions as if they were made by the hero.

VISUAL AND AUDITORY METHODS
Verbal induction methods do not work well
with very young children because their
cognitive faculties do
not develop until later.
Instead, the therapist
may ask them to fix
their gaze on a
flashlight, or use
a soothing
lullaby.

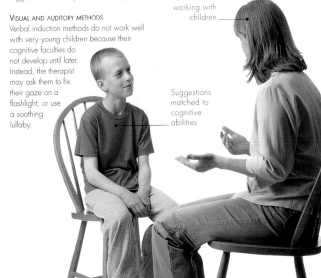

Comfortable
working with
children

Suggestions
matched to
cognitive
abilities

Relaxed
*A good rapport between the
child and therapist is essential
for an effective treatment.*

Pain Control: Hypnosis in Hospitals

Fear

It is common for children who are exposed to multiple medical procedures to become phobic about treatments.

The British psychologist and hypnotherapist John Butler, whose clinical work has included the use of hypnosis as the sole anesthetic in an abdominal hernia operation (as shown in the BBC program *Mysteries*), argues that hypnosis can make an extremely valuable contribution to the management of acute and chronic pain in children. He has taught doctors and nurses hypnoanesthesia and methods of anxiety reduction for children with a fear of doctors and medical procedures. In some hospitals it is now possible for children to be seen by pediatric nurses who have been taught to use hypnosis.

Removing fear

Hypnosis can be particularly helpful when children feel stressed about medical procedures such as repeat injections. The child may become so fearful that it is impossible to get them to the hospital for the next treatment. This is common in children with conditions such as leukemia, kidney failure, and diabetes in which blood tests are frequent and bone marrow aspiration is sometimes required. Positive suggestions using a child's imaginative capabilities can produce great improvements in the child's behavior. Teaching the parents the principles of positive suggestion in the waking state, and how to reassure and condition the child in positive ways, is also of major benefit.

Confusion and distraction techniques are often useful for children who are in pain. Direct suggestions that can be used to induce analgesia include pretending to paint numbing medicines onto the painful part of the body, giving the child a "magic spot" where no discomfort is felt during an injection, and distraction techniques such as art or play therapy, storytelling, or focusing on less uncomfortable experiences such as cold.

Observing a favorite cartoon character while in hypnosis is an excellent way for young children to relax, deepen their hypnotic experience, and distract themselves. An audiotape with a recorded therapy session or a personalized fairytale may be useful in encouraging the practice of self-hypnosis. Children over five or six can be taught to be responsible for self-hypnosis, while younger children may need a parent's active involvement to assist them.

SCIENTIFIC
INVESTIGATIONS

During the twentieth century, scientific interest in hypnosis shifted from physicians to experimental psychologists, who are more concerned with exploring its mechanisms than with documenting its therapeutic effects. ❧ In the 1950s and 1960s, one of the main areas of interest was finding out whether and why people varied in their susceptibility to hypnosis. A study in the 1950s found that students who were "well adjusted" were more susceptible than those who were not. ❧ In 1961 A.M. Weitzenhoffer and E.R. Hilgard devised the Stanford scales, which indicate how well individuals respond to suggestion and imagery. They found that, contrary to traditional belief, there is no real evidence that women are more readily hypnotizable than men. They also found that children between 8 and 12 are more hypnotizable than older or younger children.

Imaging Techniques: Measuring Electricity

EEG

The different brain waves induced in hypnosis can be recorded by electrodes attached to the scalp.

The human electroencephalogram (EEG) was first described in 1929. In the 1930s, electroencephalography—which registers potential differences on the scalp that arise as a result of electrical currents in the brain—was one of the first methods used to study hypnosis. The technique involves electrodes attached both to the scalp and to instruments that measure the brain's electrical activity in microvolts, and amplify this for recording equipment. By the frequency of the recorded activity, the EEG indicates the mental state of the subject—whether they are alert, awake, or asleep. The Greek letters alpha, beta, delta, and theta are used to describe the different wave frequencies. Different states produce different combinations of these waves. It should be noted, however, that someone under the influence of a major hallucinogen may register a normal EEG, suggesting that it is a crude indicator of changes in mental state.

In hypnosis people produce predominantly alpha waves, which indicate a relaxed state, or presleep theta waves. (Beta waves indicate alertness and delta waves indicate deep sleep.) So the pattern of brain waves recorded by EEGs has shown that the physiological state of the hypnotized person is not the same as that of the sleeping person. As James Braid observed in the nineteenth century, the muscles do not relax as in ordinary sleep and people do not drop objects held in their hands as they become more deeply hypnotized. In addition, reflexes that disappear during normal sleep can be elicited during hypnosis.

Imaging techniques

More recently, psychologists have started using modern imaging techniques to throw further light on the state of hypnosis. Magnetic resonance imaging (MRI) exploits the natural behavior of the protons (nuclei) of hydrogen atoms when they are subjected to strong magnetic fields. Positron emission tomography (PET) scans are based on the detection of positrons (positively charged electrons) that are emitted by radioactively-labeled substances introduced into the body. Both techniques can be used to reflect the metabolic and chemical activity of the different parts of the brain and how they change during hypnosis.

PET AND CAT SCANS

In the 1970s, new technology such as positron emission tomography (PET) scans and computerized axial tomography (CAT) scans examined the involvement of the right and left brain hemispheres in hypnosis. Research demonstrated a shift in activity from the left to the right hemisphere during hypnosis. The right hemisphere is associated with the creative imagination, while the left hemisphere is associated with the logical mind. Such evidence reinforces the idea that hypnosis is a change of state. It does not support the nonstate theory which argues that hypnosis is a sophisticated form of social role playing.

MRI scan

As shown by this magnetic resonance imaging (MRI) scan, during hypnosis, activity migrates from the frontal lobe to the parietal, occipital, and temporal lobes. There seems to be an emphasis on the "oldest" (in evolutionary terms) areas of the brain.

CAT scan

CAT scans show the physical structure of the brain in some detail. They are less sophisticated than MRI scans, but they are particularly useful in investigating neurological illnesses.

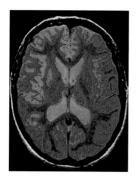

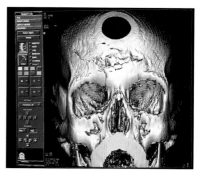

Emotion and the Brain

More recent work using MRI scans has shown that the cingulate cortex, part of the limbic system that is associated with emotional expression, becomes strongly activated during hypnosis. This suggests that hypnosis may help people to connect more powerfully with their emotions than by using relaxation alone.

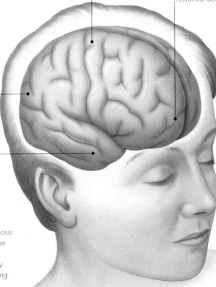

Parietal lobes, associated with one of the most abstract of neural functions, mathematics, show increased activity

Frontal lobes, associated with rational, logical processes, show reduced activity

Occipital lobes, associated with visual processing, show increased activity

Temporal lobes, concerned with language and visual imagery, show increased activity

Activity

Despite the fact that hypnosis results in feelings of intense relaxation, it produces increased activity in many areas of the brain including the temporal lobes, occipital lobes, and parietal lobes.

The Documented Effects of Hypnosis

Delicate balance
Herbert Benson's work centered on the improvement of homeostasis in hypnosis subjects.

Herbert Benson, an investigator interested in the effects of states of mind on the body, documented the health benefits of hypnosis and meditation. Working at the Beth Israel Hospital, in Boston, he measured the physiological responses in a large number of patients over many years. The details were published in his popular book *The Relaxation Response* in 1976.

Many of the changes Benson found center on improving homeostasis, the dynamic processes by which an organism maintains a constant internal environment despite external changes. In people undergoing hypnosis he found improvements in the way the body handles glucose. Such an effect may have implications for people with type II diabetes, for whom fluctuating glucose levels may lead to permanent damage to eyes, kidneys and blood vessels.

Further work showed that hypnosis reduced blood pressure, heart rate, and oxygen demand. The latter is particularly helpful since it indicates a lower rate of metabolism. This results in the reduced production of free radicals, which is significant, since free radicals are highly reactive molecules that can trigger a chain of destruction in organic molecules such as DNA. They are thought to be partly responsible for the effects of aging, and to play a role in the development of cancer. Earlier, Hans Selye, a pioneer in stress research working in Canada in the 1930s, demonstrated raised levels of corticosteroid hormones in the blood due to stress. Studies have shown that relaxation and hypnosis result in reduced levels of corticosteroids, which in turn lead to a rise in different components of the immune system.

Psychological effects

Psychological changes that have been documented during hypnosis include the reduction of forward-planning activity in the brain of the subject. A deeply hypnotized subject does not initiate activity, but tends to wait for the hypnotist to suggest things.

Selective Attention

A subject under hypnosis who is told to listen only to the hypnotist's voice will be able to block out completely any other voices in the room.

PSYCHONEUROIMMUNOLOGY

Until recently, doctors treated diseases of the mind and body as entirely separate. The relatively new field of psychoneuroimmunology seeks to explain the links between mind and body, and is throwing light on the way in which hypnosis might influence the immune system. Interest in the field was first raised in 1974 when US psychologist Robert Ader and immunologist Nicholas Cohen changed the numbers of disease-fighting T-cells in laboratory rats by using conditioning techniques. Stress was associated with a certain kind of food or drink, and relaxation with another. The T-cell counts in the rats fell in response to the stressful cues and rose in response to relaxing cues.

Rest cure

Psychological factors, such as stress and relaxation, could cause, prevent, or even be used to treat illness.

The Mind–Body Connection

The French psychiatrist Leon Chertok used hypnosis to produce experimental blisters by touching his subjects on the skin with a pen and saying "I've just touched you with a hot poker." He produced films documenting the subsequent development of a blister with a specific sequence of changes including the inflammation response. Such work provides strong evidence of the power of the mind over physiological processes.

Neuropeptides are substances which have a regulatory function in the brain, and are involved in passing messages between cells. It is now thought that they provide a link between the mind and the body.

The hypothalamus, a region of the brain the size of a cherry, has a particularly important role in mind–body interactions. Not only does it exert overall control of the sympathetic nervous system and send signals to the higher regions of the brain in response to a sudden alarm, it also connects to the pituitary gland and controls hormonal secretions into the bloodstream. Hormones released by the pituitary target the adrenal glands, ovaries, and testes through receptors that act like a "lock" for a particular hormone key to open. It is thought that cells in the immune system also have receptors that may be affected. Studies have shown that corticosteroid hormone levels rise in response to stress and that the result is a reduction in T-cell function in the immune system.

Nerve center

Developments in studies of brain structure have contributed to our understanding of common physiological responses.

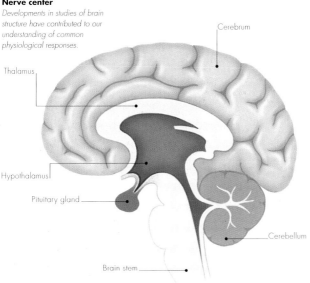

Thalamus

Cerebrum

Hypothalamus

Pituitary gland

Cerebellum

Brain stem

Ultradian Rhythms: Cycles of Consciousness

Tuned in
Ernest Rossi believed that ultradian rhythms could be used to identify the best time for hypnosis.

Ernest Rossi, a clinical psychologist who worked with Milton Erickson, developed the theory of ultradian rhythms. He proposed that the brain operates on 90-minute cycles and, at the end of this period, slows down and "takes a break." He suggests that the resting state is similar to a natural form of hypnosis. The idea is not new. The ancient Yogis claimed that there were shifts in consciousness throughout the day where breathing changed from one nostril to the other.

Ultradian rhythms have been shown to have a 90-minute "basic rest–activity cycle," which runs continuously throughout the day. They exist in addition to circadian rhythms (based on 24-hour cycles) and seasonal rhythms. It is interesting to note that the typical pattern of a working day seems to fall roughly into the 90-minute ultradian cycle, starting at 9.00 a.m. with a break at 10.30 a.m., lunch at noon, and an afternoon break at 2.30 p.m.

The signs of the rest phase in ultradian rhythms are similar to those of hypnosis. People appear to be experiencing a quiet moment of inner reflection for a few minutes, where the body becomes less active, eye blinking is reduced, and the heartbeat and respiration slows down.

The biological clock
Rossi suggested that the endocrine system (controlling hormones in the body) and the autonomic nervous

system (controlling the seemingly automatic activities of the body) are both regulated in a rhythmical manner by nerve cells in the hypothalamus, which function as biological clocks.

One theory is that psychosomatic health problems result from disruptions of the ultradian rhythms, which modulate the autonomic and endocrinological systems. Experiments have shown that when subjects are overstressed by tasks, their ultradian rhythms undergo major disruptions. The subjects experience psychosomatic conditions such as heart-rate alterations, gastritis, ulcers, asthma, and skin problems.

Rossi used hypnosis on people with health problems to accentuate the "rest" phase of the cycle, which is believed to be a natural healing time for the body. He also suggested that the restoration of ultradian rhythms may be the common factor in the beneficial effects of hypnosis, autogenic training, meditation, and the relaxation response.

GLOSSARY

Affirmations positive statements that are designed to change thinking, mood, and behavior.

Age progression guiding a hypnotized person "forward" in time so that they can see themselves in the future.

Age regression guiding a hypnotized person "backward" in time to their past.

Alpha waves the brain waves that occur in relaxed states including hypnosis, meditation, and listening to music.

Altered consciousness terminology used to refer to the state of mind we experience during hypnosis, meditation, or any form of trance.

Analgesia the inability to feel pain, even though you are fully conscious.

Anchoring establishing a trigger which, when activated, will initiate certain responses; this happens randomly in life, but can be suggested during hypnosis.

Aversion suggestion suggestions given that emphasize negative aspects of a habit, such as finding cigarette smoke repulsive.

Awakening the act of bringing a person out of a trance and in to a fully-awakened state.

Beta waves the brain waves that are produced when people are alert, awake, and aware of their surroundings.

Circadian rhythms the regular cycle your body goes through every 24 hours.

Deepening the process of using suggestions to attain a more profound trance state.

Delta waves the brain waves that occur in the dreamless state of sleep.

Desensitization behavior therapy a situation where the client is slowly and by stages brought to accept a phobic situation without fear.

Direct suggestion suggestions given as commands ("take a deep breath").

Electroencephalography the study of potential differences on the scalp that arise as a result of weak electrical currents in the brain.

Endorphins mood-altering chemicals that change the way people perceive pain.

Eye fixation induction involving staring at an object.

False memories fantasies that are experienced during a mishandled regression which are mistakenly believed to be repressed memories rather than fantasies.

Flight-or-fight reflex a primitive survival mechanism that all animals possess to get themselves out of dangerous situations.

Heterohypnosis hypnosis by another (as opposed to self-hypnosis).

Hypnosis a trance state brought about by deliberate

induction, whether by oneself or another.

Hypnotherapist a professional who uses hypnosis as an adjunct to other techniques in psychotherapy.

Hypnosis the application of hypnosis for therapeutic purposes.

Hypnotist anyone who guides another person into hypnosis.

Imagery using the imagination to fantasize or remember events.

Indirect suggestion permissive suggestions ("you can take a deep breath whenever you wish to relax").

Induction a technique the therapist uses to guide a person from the normal waking state into the hypnotic state.

Initial sensitizing event an emotional event that is the origin of a problem, such as a phobia.

Neurolinguistic Programming (NLP) an approach that helps people to utilize successful patterns of behavior to enhance their effectiveness in life.

Past life therapy regression into real or imagined past life.

Phobia a persistent irrational fear.

Posthypnotic suggestion a delayed action suggestion that operates on a hypnotized subject at a later date.

Progressive relaxation a type of induction involving the progressive relaxation of various parts of the body.

Psychoneuroimmu- nology a relatively new field that studies the links between mind and body.

Reframing using the imagination to create a different attitude to a past event.

Regression going back in time during trance to remember past events, and replaying them in the imagination, often with accompanying emotions.

Script the suggestions that the therapist uses while you are hypnotized.

Self-hypnosis a self-induced trance state.

Stage hypnosis the public use of hypnosis for entertainment purposes.

Subconscious the part of the mind that is the seat of imagination, emotion, and artistic abilities (and other skills), and which takes care of numerous functions without our conscious awareness, such as automatic functions of our organs.

Systematic desensitization exposing the client in a series of stages to the anxiety-producing stimulus while maintaining relaxation, so as to desensitize the client to the stimulus. Often used in the treatment of phobias.

Termination the therapist gives clear suggestions for the subject becoming alert.

Theta waves the brain waves that are produced the moment before you enter sleep.

Time distortion the term for a unique phenomenon where we lose conscious awareness of how much time has passed, for example 10 minutes can be made to seem like two.

Trance a state of focused concentration where you are neither asleep nor awake.

Trichotillomania the irresistible urge to pull out one's hair.

Vaginismus an involuntary and reflexive spasm of the muscles of the vagina that prevents sexual penetration.

FURTHER READING

Araoz, Daniel L. *The New Hypnosis in Sex Therapy: Cognitive–Behavioral Methods for Clinicians*, Jason Aronson, 1998.

Barrios, Alfred A. *The Habit Buster* Self-programmed Control Press, 1997

Berger, Joseph R., Miller, Caroline, Caprio, Frank Samu, and Caprio, Frank Samuel *Healing Yourself with Self-hypnosis*, Prentice Hall Direct, 1998

Bernstein, M. *The Search for Bridey Murphy*, Hutchinson, 1956.

Boys, Jennifer and Karle Hellmut, *Hypnotherapy: A Practical Handbook*, Free Association Books, 1987.

Dolan, Yvonne M. *Resolving Sexual Abuse: Solution Focused Therapy and Ericksonian Hypnosis for Adult Survivors*, W. W. Norton, 1991

Dryden, Windy and Heap, Michael *Hypnotherapy: A Handbook*, Open University Press, 1998.

Duke, Robert E. *How to Lose Weight and Stop Smoking Through Self-hypnosis*, Irvington Publishers, 1986

Fisher, Stanley *Discovering the Power of Self-hypnosis: The Simple, Natural Mind–Body Approach to Change and Healing*, Newmarket Press, 2000

Fromm, Erika *Contemporary Hypnosis Research*, Guilford Press, 1992

Gauld, Alan *A History of Hypnotism*, Cambridge University Press, 1992.

Gibson, H. B. *Hypnosis: Its Nature and Therapeutic Uses*, Peter Owen Ltd., 1977.

Greener, Mark *The Which? Guide to Managing*, Which? Consumer Guides, 1996.

Gregory, Richard L. *The Oxford Companion to the Mind*, Oxford University Press, 1995

Hadley, Josie and Staudacher, Carol *Hypnosis for Change*, New Harbinger Publications, 1996.

Hornyak, Lynne M. and Green, Joseph P. *Healing from Within: The Use of Hypnosis in Women's Health Care*, American Psychological Association, 2000

Hunter, Roy C. *Master the Power of Self-hypnosis*, Sterling Publishing Company, 1998.

Hunter, Roy C. *The Art of Hypnosis: Mastering Basic Techniques*, Kendall/Hunt Publishing Company, 2000.

IVERSEN, JEFFREY *More Lives Than One? The Evidence of the Remarkable Bloxham Tapes*, Souvenir Press, 1976.

KERSHAW, CAROL J. *The Couple's Hypnotic Dance: Creating Eriksonian Strategies in Marital Therapy*, Brunner/Mazel, 1992

KROGER, WILLIAM S. *Clinical and Experimental Hypnosis in Medicine, Dentistry, and Psychology*, Lippincott Williams and Wilkins Publishers, 1977

LECLAIRE, MICHELLE, and NEILL, O. *Creative Childbirth: The Leclaire Method of Easy Birthing Through Hypnosis and Rational-Intuitive Thought*, Papyrus Press, 1993

OVERHOLSER, LEE CHARLES *Ericksonian Hypnosis: A Handbook of Clinical Practice*, Irvington Publishers, 1984

PETERS, DAVID and WOODHAM, ANNE *Encyclopedia of Complementary Medicine*, Dorling Kindersley, 1997.

PULOS, LEE *Beyond Hypnosis*, Multimodal Press, 1990

RHUE, JUDITH W. *Handbook of Clinical Hypnosis*, American Psychological Association, 1993

ROSSI, ERNEST *The Psychobiology of Mind-body Healing*, Norton, 1986.

SANDERS, SHIRLEY *Clinical Self-hypnosis: The Power of Words and Images*, Guilford Press, 1990

SIMPKINS, ALEXANDER C. *Effective Self-Hypnosis: Pathways to the Unconscious*, Radiant Dolphins Press, 2000.

TEMES, ROBERTA *The Complete Idiot's Guide to Hypnosis*, Alpha books, 2000.

THOMAS, DOWD E. *Cognitive Hypnotherapy*, Jason Aronson, 2000

WESSON, NICKY *Alternative Maternity*, Optima, 1995.

WINTER, ALISON *Mesmerized: Powers of Mind in Victorian Britian*, The University of Chicago Press, 1998.

WYCKOFF, JAMES *Franz Mesmer: Between God and the Devil* Prentice Hall, 1975

USEFUL ADDRESSES

American Society of Clinical Hypnosis
2250 East Devon Avenue
Suite 336, Des Plaines
Illinois 60018
Tel: 312 645 9810

American Psychological Association: Division 30
For information about hypnosis, see www.apa.org/about/division/div30.html, or call 800 374 2721 or 202 336 5500

Milton H. Erickson Foundation
1935 East Aurelius Avenue,
Phoenix, Arizona 85850
www.ericksonfoundation.org

National Guild of Hypnotists, Inc
For information on how to locate practitioners, see www.ngh.net, or call 603 429 9433

International Medical and Dental Hypnotherapy Association
For a hypnotherapy directory by state, see www.infinityinst.com/index.html, or call 800 257 5467

Institute for Complementary Medicine
PO Box 194,
London SE16 7QZ, UK
Tel: 020 7237 5165
Fax: 020 7237 5175

British Society of Medical and Dental Hypnosis (Scotland)
PO Box 1007
Glasgow, G31 2LE, UK
Tel: (0141) 5561606

British Society of Hypnotherapists (1950)
37 Orbain Road,
London SW6 7JZ, UK
Tel: (020) 7385 1166
email: sy@bsh1950.fsnet.co.uk

British Psychological Society (BPS)
St Andrews House
48 Princess Road East
Leicester LE1 7DR, UK
Tel: (0116) 254 9568
Fax: (0116) 247 0787
www.bps.org.uk

British Association of Counselling (BAC)
1 Regent Place
Rugby, Warwickshire
CV21 2PJ, UK
Tel: (01788) 550899
Fax: (01788 562189)
www.counselling.co.uk

United Kingdom Council of Psychotherapy (UKCP)
167-9 Great Portland Street
London W1N 5FB, UK
Tel: (020) 7436 3002
Fax: (020) 7436 3013
www.psychotherapy.org.uk

British Complementary Medicine Association (BCMA)
249 Fosse Road South
Leicester LE3 1AE, UK
Tel: (0116) 282 5511

INDEX

ACKNOWLEDGMENTS

The publisher would like to thank
Deborah Fielding for reading and commenting
on the text.

PICTURE ACKNOWLEDGMENTS

AKG, London 38l, 40, 101, 186l/ Eric Lessing 31t; **The Bridgeman Art Library** /
Musee des Beaux-Arts, Orleans, France 106b / Private Collection 41, 113 / Victoria & Albert
Museum, London UK 37; **Bulls Press** 179; **Corbis** 27tr, 187l / Bettmann Archive 30l, 35,
36, 43t, 156, 185 / Ales Fewzer 178b / Mitchell Gerber 187tr / Hulton Getty 23t / James
Marshall 66 / Diego Lezama Orezzoli 89 / Gianni Dagli Orti 22 / Underwood & Underwood
184·/ Roger Wood 23b; **Mary Evans** 107; **Hulton Getty** 20, 25, 33; **The Image
Bank** / Barros & Barros 130b / David Gould 142t / Lars Klove 114t; **Images Colour
Library** 94b, 98t, 106t, 110b, 134t, 154, 200; **Rex Features** 39b / John Borrowman 39t;
Dr Ernest Rossi 212; **Science Photo Library** 24 / Jean-Loup Charmet 27tl, 27b; **The
Stock Market** / Rob Lewine 122t; **Tony Stone Images** 98b, 114, 150 / Tim Brown 158
/ Pascal Crapet 196 / Scott Cunningham 74b / Davies & Starr 96 / Lonnie Duka 182b /
Laurence Dutton 206l / Sean Ellis 86b / David Hanover 142b / Frank Herholdt 174 / David
Job 138t / Charles Krebs 110t / Tom Landecker 201 / Philip Lee Harvey 74t / Mark Lewis 188
/ Anthony Marsland 210 / Trevor Mein 50t / Denis O'Clair 138b / David Oliver 182t / Frank
Orel 92 / Michael Rosenfield 204 / David Roth 65 / Stephanie Rushton 117 / Richard Shock
206r / Timothy Shonnard 102b, 116 / Charles Thatcher 162 / Bob Thomas 176 / Mitch
Tobias 94t / Bob Torrez 194 / Julie Toy 105 / John Turner 148 / Terry Vine 9 / Stuart
Westmorland 43b / Stuart Young Reiss 168; **Werner Forman** / Denver Art Museum,
Colorado, USA 42t / Centennial Museum, Vancouver, Canada 42b.